Interior Design for Profit

by
Mary V. Knackstedt
ASID/NHFL

KOBRO PUBLICATIONS, INC.
New York, N.Y.

Edited By: Laura J. Haney
Printed in the United States

ISBN 0-9604676-0-2

Library of Congress Catalog Card Number 80-82858

For all Interior Designers, crafts people and trade sources committed to create environments where people enjoy working and living.

Credits and Acknowledgments

Grateful thanks are due to:

Dr. John O. Hershey and John Aichele, clients and special friends. They taught me that a designer who wishes to sell to business and professional people must approach them in a businesslike manner, with a business vocabulary.

Ed Luck, who inspired Sunday night business dinners where the problems of the week were discussed and ways of handling them suggested.

Bud Pease of Payne and Co., who made me understand that selling and profit must be the prime colors in the designer's palette.

Bert Laudenslager, Coleman Witte, Pedro Rodriguez of my Pennsylvania East chapter, and the many people on the national ASID scene, for their encouragement. Alby Phibbs, self-styled cheerleader, stands out because he let me know that what I was doing had some value.

Bernie Halkin, who first used the term "The Twilight Zone" to refer to client relationships in our yearly ASID workshops on professional practices.

The many designers and business advisors who shared with me their procedures and practices, and the many who attended the workshops. These workshops brought to my attention the different issues that are presented in this book: a composition of ideas and attitudes that were gathered from the workshops.

Lovinia Buckwalter, my speech teacher for over 16 years, who prepared me with the verbal skills that are a necessary part of the workshops.

Arlene Palitz who helped with much of the interaction and administration between the publishers and my office. Her support and managerial expertise are most appreciated.

Laura J. Haney who encouraged me and edited this book.

THE DESIGNER magazine, where some of this material was first published. My staff and associates, for working with me to make our company more profitable.

CONTENTS

Introduction

I feel it is immoral to lose money. If you lose money, then you start to take short cuts on projects. The client is a loser, you are a loser, everyone loses. For any field to be worth putting our life and energy into, we must have rewards for our efforts. You must be able to pay your daily expenses without having to worry excessively. If you are going to spend all your time worrying where the next dollar is coming from and how the jobs will pay, then you will not be as creative a designer as you would like.

Reviewing the income level of interior designers who attend my Interior Design for Profit seminars, I found that the annual income is low considering the years we spend in academic study, the years in apprenticeship, and the hours we work.

We must understand basic business principles or we are forced to work under people who do. Whether we work independently, directly under someone, or have hired financial people, we should understand some of the procedures, values and attitudes of finance and business. Knowing a simple business vocabulary is a requirement in order to run the simplest interior design firm today. If we are employed in a larger firm, understanding where the company is going financially increases our value to the firm.

This book is intended for the student, the young designer and the person who has been in business many years yet wants a basic comparison. These attitudes and profit procedures are some that I pulled from businesses other than interior design, as well as from interior design firms.

This book is written in a very simple fashion because I feel, as do many other people who have successfully run small business, that the key is to keep procedure as simple as possible. Often, MBA's create such involved procedures that the entrepreneurs and creative planners within the company no longer understand the profit structures set up for their firms.

Interior Design for Profit is suited for anyone from the single designer to employees of a company up to approximately five million in gross sales, although employees of larger firms may find many points of this book profitable.

Interior design is a profession. Everything you do as a designer must relate to it. The way you design and the way you use design concepts form an art. The way you deal with clients, contractors, manufacturers and employees in a business also requires a structure in order for it be profitable.

What is the sign on your door? Is it to make a profit? Interior design is my art and my profession. It is also my business and livelihood. I do not expect the money from one job to carry me for the year. I have to show a percentage of profit in each job in order to have a reasonable profit at the end of the year.

Even if interior design is strictly a hobby for you, if you consider interior design a business, remember that a business must make a profit.

I have been in the interior design business since 1958. Although I wish it were my hobby, I have ended up responsible for 11 employees, each of whom has a family, medical needs, physical needs and desires. I feel responsible for the success and growth of the firm. I know that it depends upon the goals, attitudes and planning of its principal. During the last twenty years, I have observed many other businesses, their procedures and problems. I have read a great deal and attended many, many workshops on the subject of business practices.

Running an interior design firm today is not simple. My father had a furniture manufacturing business for some 39 years. If he could see the type of business procedures we are dealing with today, I am sure he would never believe that this is the same general business.

We are involved with so many things—taxes, loans, contracts, the issues of billing procedures and inflation— that were not so crucial ten years ago.

I have found in my business that the areas in which I am losing money are often subtle ones, the ones you would not expect to need watching, such as increase of cost of merchandise, which has become a major thing. This was not an important point ten years ago. The cost of maintaining inventory is now excessive, far beyond what we can normally mark up our inventory each year. Property costs and utilities have become a major item for everyone renting or owning property. Freight and handling, once considered a minor expense on any job now often eats up a major portion of the profits. You must watch each area very carefully in order to be assured that you are not making it in one point and losing in another.

QUESTIONS ONE MIGHT ASK ONESELF WHEN CONSIDERING A CAREER IN THE INTERIOR DESIGN FIELD

1. How important is the field of interior design to you?
2. What kind of life style do you want to lead?
3. Do you want to be identified as an interior designer?
4. How much time do you want to devote to the field?
5. Are you willing to spend the time and money required for the formal training needed?
6. Do you feel you have the innate artistic abilities to become a success?
7. Do you like the people in the field enough to work with them?
8. Do you have the personality to work with clients?
9. Do you enjoy planning and organizing?
10. Are you self-disciplined?
11. Are you self-motivated?

Personal Goals
and Business Goals

Each of us has personal needs and desires. Whatever your desires, you cannot deny them if you are going to be happy and fulfilled. Our personal goals are largely dependent upon obtaining certain business objectives; it is vital to carefully correlate the two. Do your personal goals fit realistically with the interior design field?

In working and talking with other interior designers, I have found that many use the field as an avocation rather than an occupation. In fact, over 30% of the people who attend my profit workshop do not rely on the interior design field for financial security.

I consider interior design an art; I would like to feel it s a sacred one. For many of us it is also a business. It is a reative one, but it still must be run profitably.

It is good to sit down and take stock as to how you actually feel about the interior design field, even if you do not do this at the beginning of your career. How important is it to you? Is it something you want to spend the rest of your life doing? Or is it something you must want to dabble in for several years to gain experience and then perhaps go on to another field? At this time, it is important to put your private thoughts into perspective.

Your personal goals are not necessarily the goals of your family or your clients. Be honest with yourself in setting these goals to insure that they correlate with your business goals.

We have learned that many workaholics really enjoy what they are doing. For them work is not work, but play and fun and a thrilling, exciting experience. I feel it is wrong to condemn someone who enjoys what they do. But there is some truth to the psychologists' claim that being a workaholic leads to burn-out. Many social scientists believe we need physical activity and other types of stimuli outside our professional experience.

After burn-out there really is no going back to exactly what we had before. A vacation sometimes can help but it really never puts us back into our former position. The important thing is to avoid this and to work to avoid this from the very day you begin your profession. Decide what kind of a balance you need and just what is important to you and create that balance.

A good way to define your personal goals is to decide where you see yourself five years from now, so I have adjusted my personal plan to reach my business goals. I have had to revise this many times, but at least I have a goal pattern. It makes me feel more secure to think that I am ruling and running my life, rather than that I am a victim of my life.

6

How do you evaluate your personal goals? Each of us knows more about ourselves than anyone else in the world. You know what you like and dislike, you know what things work best for you and how you work best with other people. You know if you like to live alone or whether you like to live with other people and how much you value your professional field. You also know your financial requirements, whether you want to live in border-line poverty or whether you require more comforts that finances must purchase. Determine how much you want to live with and how much you can do without.

You can learn more about yourself by outlining these goals. List making and outlining gives us a tremendous amount of system and organization required for the business world today. I begin each day with a list of goals and outline what I expect to complete on that day. Although I may not always complete them, I am sure that lists help me to accomplish a few more of these goals than would have been possible without them.

For your goal-setting process, sit down and decide what is important to you. Then, make another list of the things that really annoy you, the things that you do not enjoy, the things that you really want to stay away from. This is probably something you can do yourself or with another person. Sharing some of these goals and objectives with other professionals or friends can often enlighten you. They can help you by reminding you of certain personal preferences that you may not have considered.

Consider the responsibilities that you have for yourself. Do I feel good about my work? The people in my life? Myself? Do I waste valuable time and energy on things that really do not matter?

List at least a half a dozen activities that you enjoy doing purely for fun and the last time you had an opportunity to do some of these things. If it has been a very long time, perhaps something is wrong with your life plan. If the idea of doing something that is bigger or better causes you to work harder and perhaps without much joy or excitement, what should you be doing differently to make you happier? More productive? Less frustrated and bored? These answers can prove to be an adventure in self-discovery. If you have an unrealistic expectation, you created it for yourself.

It is a good idea to review your goals every 3 to 6 months to be sure they can be accomplished. If you find that you have not accomplished some, it is a clue that you have the wrong diagram.

In order to maintain professionalism, we must constantly recharge our enthusiasm. It is important to plan some quiet time alone to reset your direction and sometimes to reward yourself for finishing a bothersome job.

Personal goals and business goals must carefully be coordinated. Each design firm ought to review its financial goals as well as its design goals once a year, with monthly reviews, to be sure the firm is going in the right direction.

What is the sign on your door? Is it to make a profit? Many interior design firms with beautifully designed offices are really not in business to make a profit. They do not have to . . . they have incomes from other sources. But, is that really a business?

A good business plan projects approximately five years into the future. Many business plans cannot be completed within one or two years, but require three to five years.

One of the problems of small business is that we are so busy taking care of the day-to-day problems that we do not spend much time planning toward our business objectives.

8

The reason so many companies never accomplish their goals is that they are not really sure what they are in the first place and, secondly, they have not organized their efforts in this direction.

Review your business goals with your accountant, your business consultant and your attorney. I have had what I thought were very exciting business plans for my company, only to find after reviews with my CPA that some of these plans meant simply that I would pay most of the money in taxes. Your goals may change from year to year, depending upon your financial situation and even different tax rulings.

Define the objectives of your business plans very clearly to determine just how this fits with your personal goals as well as those of your employees. Is your plan a simple one? If you get too complex, it will be hard for other people to understand your plan or to work with you to attain it.

Be flexible. We are creative in our work of interior design, so we must be creative in our plan for business goals.

Procrastination can ruin any business goal. Review your business goals every few months. If you have not accomplished a portion of these goals, perhaps you should go back and revise them. They might be the wrong goals for your company.

Learn to balance large important decisions against the unimportant. Consider the big picture of your goals, where you want to be five years from now. Allow time in your regular schedule for planning and effectively developing these goals. Do not spend all your time putting out fires, make sure you are working toward the goals you have established.

How To Get The Position
You Want

With the right research, it is reasonably possible for anyone to get the job he really wants. I recommend, before you invest several years of your life with a firm, that you investigate in detail the kind of work they do. Chances are that as a new member of the company, you are not going to be able to change it much. You will have to fit in with their design format. Is it the environment in which you will be happy?

You investigate the type of work a design firm does by looking at publications (trade, consumer, books), by asking people who worked with them about the projects they worked on, or by approaching the firm directly. You do not necessarily have to say why you are interested in the firm. You might say simply that you admire their work and would like the opportunity to see more of it. Most design firms are proud of their work and will happily tell you about their projects. Visiting the project will tell you something about the quality of the firm.

Ask questions about each of the major people within the company. Find out their education and business backgrounds. It helps to know that one man has an architectural background; another, interior design; that one has specialized in hospitals, another in graphic arts. This information is available through other designers, through their clients, and companies they have worked with. It is wise to run a credit check on the company to learn about their financial situation and to get an idea of their growth pattern. Where did they start, and how long did it take to reach their present status?

Anyone seeking employment should be familiar with the firm he wants to work for. The first thing I ask any prospective employee is, "What do you know about our company?" When someone says he saw the name in the Yellow Pages, I am not really impressed. I feel that if this person did not care enough to research the firm, to be sure she really wants to invest the next few years of her life working with us, why should I want to make her part of our team?

After one of my lectures, a senior student at Philadelphia Textile School came to me for advice on how to get a job in textile arts in her home state of Colorado. She had found that most of the textile arts positions were in the northeastern United States around New York and Philadelphia. I asked what she meant by no jobs. Wasn't there even *one* company?

Yes, she admitted, there was one specializing in fabrics for male and female ready-to-wear clothing, but she didn't know much about them other than that they had a

12

large factory, had been in the same location a number of years, and said they had no openings when she had asked.

I then asked her what her father did for a living. Since he was in insurance, I pointed out that he would know a lot of people in the community and could find out about the major people in the firm and their backgrounds. "You want to know how long they have been with the company," I said. "You want to know about families, whether they live within the community or whether they commute from a distance—anything you can find out about how these people relate to this company."

I suggested a research project for her to do at the same time: she should use her Saturdays and free days to visit major stores and department stores in the eastern part of the state and talk to the buyers about how they felt about that particular textile company. She should create an outline of appropriate questions and ask them of every buyer: whether they liked the quality, which colors sold better, which year the line was best . . . It would take about six months to accumulate the information to put into a professional presentation.

After this was completed, she should test the presentation, polish it—refine it. Then, as I suggested, she called the president of the firm when she went home for Christmas vacation. She told him she had spent six months doing research on his company, then asked for an appointment to review it with him. She got the appointment. He was surprised she was so interested in his firm, and he was interested in some of the comments she brought him, which differed from what his staff had told him. It is hard to know just what he was most impressed by, but the main thing is that he *was* impressed by the attention she had given his company. She told him of her textile arts training and that she intended to move back to Colorado and would like to work in his company.

Of course, the president was aware of her interest. He didn't know what job he was going to give her, but she was hired. He told her to come back in June and he would have something for her then. The head of the textile art department would be retiring in 18 months. If she continued to maintain her interest in the firm, he felt she might work into that job.

If we put the care into planning our futures that we put into our interior designs, we can have the things we want out of life. No one can expect to have the perfect job handed to him. We can plan for and plot and go after the job we want and really should have, and if we do it in a professional manner, we will get it.

It is important, in selecting someone to work for, to find someone you can accept as your mentor, someone whose advice you are willing to follow and work with and really become part of for a considerable period of time. According to an article in the NEW YORK magazine, where heads of corporations, law firms, and banks were interviewed about the single factor that helped them to attain their positions, each and every one of them had a mentor.

In my opinion, it can be suicide for a young designer to go independent too soon. If you want to build a career, find someone whose work you admire. *Find yourself a mentor.*

Starting a New Firm

A new business has a 5% chance of succeeding. Half of all new businesses last less than two years. One out of three lasts less than four years. One in five lasts more than ten years.

Many people who start a business do not realize that even a small business requires good management. In fact, lack of good management and insufficient capital are the two most frequently cited reasons for business failure.

Since bookkeeping, money management and finance are generally the bugaboos of designers, one of the first things to do is to acquire the services of a good accountant who will not only help set up a bookkeeping system, but will explain how to determine capital requirements, among other things. A business consultant could be helpful with the above. A banker can be of help in securing any necessary loan and in other financial matters.

Before enlisting the help of either banker or accountant, know your potential market. Find out who your competitors are and what services you can offer that will be different. A town that is largely residential, for example, may need several designers who work in that area, but there will also be medical offices, stores, schools and hospitals that need design services. On the other hand, in a large urban area, these contract jobs may predominate. Find out if there is a place for you.

Acquire an image. Once you know the type of business you are going after, it is important to create a design image that will appeal to that clientele, while retaining your versatility. A thorough knowledge of sources, contractors, and resources of all types is another pre-business requirement.

Is the population of the community increasing or decreasing? Perhaps some industry plans to move into the area. That would create a need for offices, schools, residences, and would open up many opportunities for design.

How much will it cost to run an office in this area? It used to be said that the occupancy cost of opening a store or an office should not exceed five percent of the anticipated gross sales. The cost of properties and rentals has escalated tremendously, so it is doubly important to be cautious about property costs being in line with potential profits.

Do you have the personal qualifications for running a business? Here are some questions you should ask yourself.

1. Is creating a business and seeing it grow important to you?
2. Are you a well organized person?
3. Are you doing well in your present position? What are your strong points, weak points?

16

4. Are you making money for your present employer? Have you considered merging with him or her?
5. Can you make major decisions easily? If you are not comfortable making decisions, your own business may cause too much aggravation.
6. Do you usually make the right decision?
7. Are you afraid of failure?
8. Are you willing to risk everything for the future? Running a business continually entails risk.
9. Are you strong in all areas of business? If not, do you plan to have associates or other supporting personnel who will cover you in your weak areas?
10. Do you have enough self-motivation? Since there will be no one to tell you what to do, it is important to be motivated to plan and expedite the various responsibilities of a business.
11. Can you motivate others? Have you managing ability?
12. When you start something, do you follow through? Dropping a job before it is completed is a common weakness. It is exciting to begin a project but there are many nasty details to attend to toward the end.
13. Can you organize and plan a project from beginning to end? If you don't have organizing ability, which is essential for expediting projects, you should consider hiring someone to handle this.
14. Can you handle money well? Personal experience will probably give you the answer to this.
15. Are you willing to work long hours? A new business requires a lot of time and effort. Since it is your business you are usually the one who must attend to many of the little fringe areas which no one can be hired to do. This takes a lot more time than you have been devoting to your design work.
16. Are you physically capable of running your own

business? It will take a lot more stamina than working for someone else would. If not, you may be better off employed by others or at least having several associates.

If you are satisfied with your qualifications and have decided to set up your own business, ask yourself if your master plan is viable. It should include everything from marketing to expediting your jobs. Your overall business plan should be reviewed by professional advisors: your attorney, your accountant, and perhaps your financial advisor.

YOUR OFFICE

Deciding on an office location is first a question of where property is available and space suitable for your interior design operation. Consider whether it is convenient to your markets. This may save time searching for materials. You may want your office to be close to your home or to the homes of people who will be working with you.

Parking, public transportation, and neighborhood stability are important. Check the insurance rates for the area too.

How does the community feel about having you there? If the answer is negative, it will probably be more trouble than it is worth.

Check the cost of utilities. This has become extremely important in recent years. Several designers have been forced to move because of escalating utility costs. Taxes also can be a staggering part of today's overhead.

Space is expensive but it varies from one location to another. It is therefore difficult to set any general rule as to what you should spend or whether you would be better off with more or less space.

Whether to build, buy an existing building, or rent, is entirely based on your needs and the amount of capital you have available. Putting too much capital into real estate and thereby limiting your working capital is a common error. Your choices, however, are limited to what is available. Consider the length of time you will probably stay in a location and invest in it accordingly. It is foolish to put a lot of money into remodeling an existing property or building a new one if you are not going to stay there for a reasonable length of time. Any location you consider must be reviewed financially by your accountant and your banker. They will give you guidelines which will be extremely important in your design.

If you decide to rent, remember that most commercial leases provide for rent increases based on rises in real estate taxes, operating expenses, cost of living, or a combination of these. Have the landlord outline the real estate taxes and any other expenses you will be required to pay.

In many leases the tenant is required to pay a portion of the operating expenses of the building. This is particularly true of shopping center leases. Have it stated at the beginning whether you or the landlord are responsible for general maintenance and just what the charges will be. Operating expenses include accounting fees, management, advertising, and special expenses befitting a single tenant. The tenant should ask for a ceiling on this type of rent increase. Have someone who knows real estate review the lease.

If you decide to build, remember that as a designer you will put a lot of time and effort into the project. Can you afford the time away from other design projects? This time should be scheduled, just as you would do for a client's project. Your own building should be the epitome of what you are selling. The product is design, so spare no effort in its creation.

STARTING A NEW BUSINESS EXPENSES

Start-Up - One Time	$28,250.00
6 Month Overhead @ $3,840.00	23,040.00
6 Month Salary - Designer $24,000 per year Assistant $12,000 per year	18,000.00

Total Budget Needed
to start a new business $69,290.00 to
                                                     80,000.00

START-UP WORKSHEET — ONE TIME COSTS

Rental - Security deposit - 2 months	$ 900.00
Furnishings - including drafting table, typewriter, copymachine, phone answering device, furniture required	10,000.00
Initial drafting and presentation supplies	1,000.00
Office supplies	1,500.00
Stationery and brochure	2,500.00
Signs and graphics	1,000.00
Announcement, promotion expenses	5,000.00
Telephone installation	
Legal and accounting start-up charges	2,000.00
Library - samples, catalogues that must be purchased, reference books necessary	4,000.00
	$28,250.00

The expenses on this list are generally one time expenses. However, they are expenses that one must have cash for in advance of starting a business. They will vary considerably depending upon the locale and your general presentation required.

RENTAL SECURITY DEPOSIT

Assuming you rent your first studio instead of purchasing, a two-month security deposit is needed.

FURNISHINGS

Your initial office costs will be much greater if you plan to use your office for presentation work. Any design office should be furnished in a way that is representative of your design quality. The expense could be considerable. It is an area where a designer should use as much creativity as possible to attempt to keep this cost down. It is more important to have cash available for the working expenses of the firm. Before you determine what you are going to spend on furniture, decide just how much you will be using this office and establish a budget accordingly. This budget does include all your drafting tables, typewriters, answering phones, answering devices, furniture required, copying machines.

OFFICE SUPPLIES

Some office equipment can be purchased on time: dictating machines and adding machines, for instance. You might be able to cut expenses by borrowing or purchasing second-hand but still workable office machines.

STATIONERY AND BROCHURE

Our stationery and brochures should represent our design quality. I suggest that you hire a professional graphic designer to do it for you. It is expensive since we require something of good quality, and it will take a lot of design study to be sure that the graphic presentation truly represents the designer's image.

SIGNS AND GRAPHICS

Depending upon your location, you may need a certain number of signs. I think that signage should be kept to a minimum and done in good taste.

ANNOUNCEMENT AND PROMOTION EXPENSE

The initial announcement and promotion expense probably is one of the larger promotion expenses of the design studio, but it is needed.

TELEPHONE INSTALLATION

At one time a minimal cost, telephone installation is an expensive item that must be budgeted. Keep phone service to a minimum in starting an office. As your office grows, you can always increase the telephone service.

LEGAL AND ACCOUNTING START-UP CHARGES

Legal and accounting start-up charges can be given to you by your attorney and your accountant. It will vary considerably depending upon the professional you use. It is crucial, however, at this point to be sure you have good legal and accounting direction. It is necessary to get an outline from them early in the game or before starting your business to be sure you have outlined and covered all the requirements for your type of business.

LIBRARY, SAMPLES, CATALOGS
THAT MUST BE PURCHASED

For each business, whether it be contract or residential, there are a number of samples, catalogs and reference material that is required. Much of this must be purchased because some of the better things are just not given away to new businesses. Of course, we try to collect as much as we can free, but what we can't, we must buy. We need good reference material. This belongs in your budget, because you will not have the time to go out researching every item you need for each job.

You may have accumulated a number of reference books through the years. However, there are certain reference materials such as architectural and graphic standards which you will want to be sure to have.

FIRST SIX MONTHS SALARIES AND EXPENSES

Refer to the general budget sheet and allow six months expenditures. The reason for the six-month period is because the turnover of cash in the interior design business is slower than other professional businesses because basically we must acquire the client, we must do the design, we must fill it and get paid. Even if we are paid on a monthly basis, a six-month period is a very short one for this turnover. The more comfortable period would be one year. However, if we have covered all the other expenses and are positive of having six months' funds and see a considerable amount of work projected, this will be sufficient.

OVERHEAD EXPENSES FOR ONE MONTH

Approximate - based on designer with one assistant

Support Staff	40% non-billable	
	$12,000 per year	$ 400.00
Fringe benefits, holidays, etc.		
Rent, including light, heat		450.00
Telephone		200.00
Automotive		300.00
Insurance		350.00
Maintenance		60.00
Office and Studio Expenses, Postage		120.00
Sample Expenses		200.00
Travel and Entertainment		300.00
Accounting and Legal		100.00
Marketing (Designer or staff person's salary for time spent marketing; 30% of time for a $24,000 per year person)		700.00
Interest		- 0 -
Dues and Subscriptions		70.00
Taxes and Licenses		440.00
Depreciation		420.00
Contributions		30.00
TOTAL		$4,240.00

Marketing is part of the foundation of a company. Therefore, I like to see it included as a fixed overhead expense.

Structuring Your Firm

Operating an interior design firm in the 1980's is considerably different from managing one in the past. There are going to be many changes in the structure in which interior designers are working. One of the forms of business I think will be very strong in the 80's is a partnership or corporation similar to that which attorneys and physicians use.

Interior designers do not compete with each other, but with professionals in other disciplines. By working together in a partnership we can establish and use the same libraries, sample sources, the same secretarial and business organizational forces, the same financial structure, and combine marketing efforts. This type of organization could bring strength to many individual designers who are working independently now, especially since we are in a creative art where interaction so often spurs inspiration.

A number of such firms are being established throughout the country.

Expediting jobs is an issue which requires management talent more than interior design talent. I feel that there will be many expediting companies established— companies that will do nothing but manage and expedite jobs, whether they be large or small. It would permit the interior designer to concentrate his efforts in the areas in which he is trained and to polish the project.

As designers, we realize that the weak part of the job can ruin our professional esteem with our client. This weakness often is due to improper business management. It is crucial to establish and structure a design firm according to good business principles in order to have the best expediting procedures on jobs.

It is often said that 10% of the job involves the design and 90% of the job involves expediting. We were all trained in the 10% but not in the 90%. So perhaps it is a good professional procedure to turn this over to someone who is familiar with the management and expediting procedures rather than just interior design.

PROPRIETORSHIP

There are basically three forms of business ownership. The sole proprietorship is easy to establish. The owner begins and automatically he is a sole proprietor. All profits earned by the business belong to the owner, who has total authority over his business structure. There are few legal restrictions with the sole proprietorship except the general areas of civil and criminal law, which apply to all forms of ownership.

There are some disadvantages. The owner must come up with the total capital that is required for the business.

The life of the business depends totally on the owner. If the owner decides to close his door—and he can do this at any time—the business ceases to exist.

The owner also has unlimited liability. He is liable, not only for the amount that he has invested, but all his other assets. In the case of a bankruptcy or legal judgment, all the assets, with the exception of his homestead and other things that are specified by state law, can be taken from him to satisfy the legal claims against his company.

PARTNERSHIP

A partnership consists of two or more people and may be established on almost any basis that the partners choose. Although a formal agreement is not legally required for partners, it is suggested that a legal document called The Articles of Co-Partnership be drawn up to establish what authority each person has, how the profit and loss of the company is to be shared. If one is not established the state usually requires that the distribution of authority, profit and loss be equal.

There are two types of partnership: General Partner and Limited Partner. There must be at least one *general partner*. This person has unlimited liability. He may be held liable, not just to the extent of the investment in the business, but also any other assets he may have. The general partner must be active in the operations of the business.

You need not have any *limited partners*, but there is no limit to the number a partnership may have. The principal difference between a general partner and a limited partner is that the limited partner has limited liability. The limited partner can lose his investment in the partnership but other assets that he might have cannot be touched.

‸ limited partner may or may not take active part in ʔgement of the business.

ᵌ four classifications of limited partnership. ᴵⁿᵉ ᵌʳ is one who takes an active part in the managemenᵗ ᵒ‿ ᵁusiness but it is not known that he is a partner. If it becomes ρublicly known, then he is considered a general partner in terms of liability.

The *silent partner* is known to the public but has no voice in the operations of the firm. He must divorce himself from all partnership business and operations.

The *dormant partner* is unknown to the public and is absolved from any part of the management of the partnership.

The *nominal partner* is not an owner of the business, but lends his name for a fee or consideration. He does not take part in the operation of the business. This could be a famous designer or someone else who allows you to use his name without any part of the business.

There are many advantages to the partnership form of ownership. It requires very little effort and it is not costly to establish. Usually, the only cost is the legal fee for drawing up and recording the Articles of Co-Partnership. Usually, there is more money available when two or more people begin a business.

In a partnership, it allows for limited partnerships who have limited liability. Many types of relationships can be established within a partnership. This often permits people of different talents and skills to enter a business. With designers, it can be a merging of different talents within the interior design field or including people of similar arts such as architecture, landscape architecture, engineering, lighting and business management.

30

Restrictions for a partnership are usually similar to that of proprietorship. One of the principal disadvantages to a partnership is that a partnership does not spell out as clearly as a corporation the responsibilities of different partners. There can be areas of overlapping authority and conflicts can develop.

Partnerships do not have the ability for accumulating capital the corporation has. There is considerably more liability to a partnership than to a corporation. If a member of the partnership should drop out, the partnership automatically ceases.

THE CORPORATION

Corporation is a form of ownership of three or more people who are known as stockholders. A corporation is created as a legal being that may own property and enter into contracts, be liable for debt, sue and be sued, and conduct day-to-day business. In order to become a corporation, you must obtain a charter from the state. Different states have different requirements for establishing a corporation.

Capital for the corporation is accumulated by selling stock. There are two types of stock: preferred and common. The principal advantage of a corporation is that it can accumulate capital subject to the rate of corporate tax within each state, which is usually considerably less than the individual income rate.

The life of a corporation, which is established in its charter, can continue beyond the individual stockholder's involvement by simply selling the stock to another owner. The corporation also has limited liability, which means that the stockholders are liable principally for the value of the stock that they have invested.

There are some exceptions to this. Today when a corporation borrows money on a legal obligation, most financial institutions require the individuals to co-sign the acquired obligation. In most instances, today when someone plans to sue a corporation, he is also going to sue the primary officers of that corporation.

There are some disadvantages to establishing a corporation. One is that it is more expensive and it takes a greater length of time. The cost of attorney fees as well as state fees are much greater than the other two forms of companies.

The tax situation can be an advantage for some and a disadvantage for others. This should be discussed carefully with your accountant before determining if it is to your advantage to establish a corporation.

There are many more restrictions on corporations. The state and government require many regular reports to various agencies. The cost of accounting and expediting of all these forms and details can prove to be very expensive.

For determining which type of business is proper for your company, carefully review this with your attorney, your accountant, and your business consultant. Many companies have incorporated quickly only to find it to be a great disadvantage to them because of the expense involved in mantaining the accounting procedures, as well as some tax situations which are not always profitable.

There is also a *Subchapter S Corporation.* This is a business that has filed for corporate status at the state level and enjoys the benefits, but the firm makes the selection with IRS that it does not want to be taxed like a corporation but would rather be treated as a partnership. It must be established in advance with IRS. If a corporation decided to terminate its Subchapter S position, there is usually the restriction that you cannot reapply for approximately five years for Subchapter S status. This must be carefully planned with your accountant before determining whether this is profitable for you.

There are many advantages to this type of corporation. If a company makes a profit, the corporation does not have to pay any tax on it and this eliminates one of the very large drawbacks of corporate ownership. If a company should have a loss, these can also be passed on to the shareholders and can be taken as a loss on their personal returns.

Business Development

To maintain your business activity three years from now, you have got to seek new business now. The business practice of marketing is an effective tool for controlling short-, middle- and long-term development. Most designers are educated in professional design, but they are not educated as business people.

Marketing involves far more than promotion. It requires an involved understanding of all the tasks to be undertaken for public visability and for client rapport.

The first and most important part of the practice of marketing is to establish your company's overall goals. Once you know your direction, it is easier to delineate intermediate objectives. It is then possible to identify the strategies needed to achieve each objective, and the tactics required to accomplish the final steps can be identified and applied.

At one time, it was thought that marketing was selling a product to a client. Today, marketing is a question of who needs the product. Is it saleable? Is the client ready for this product or service at this particular time? A professional designer, with limited funds, should pinpoint the marketing area. It is quite costly to blanket the field; even a large design firm cannot afford to do this. The most costly mistake that marketers make is to place the entire emphasis on the clients or prospective clients and to overlook in-house capabilities.

The first part of a designer's marketing program is to analyze in-house abilities. Is the firm capable of carrying to completion the accomplishments of a projects that it is attempting to acquire? Review what the design firm has done in the past, what it is doing now, and what it hopes to do in the future.

To do this, make a complete outline of the personnel within the firm and analyze the staff's abilities, accomplishments and goals. (There is a sample questionnaire later in the chapter.) Then correlate this with the company's goals.

Your market is loosely defined as the total of those individuals or organizations who need and want the services that a professional interior designer can supply and are willing and able to pay for these services.

ESTABLISHING THE DESIGN FIRM'S GOALS

Begin with the principals of the firm. They must agree on exactly what the firm's goals are. Possible goals might be growth, increasing profit, increasing the rate of profit, increasing your market share.

Growth is the key to many business endeavors. The future of a company depends on its flexibility and the

willingness to grow. Attaining many other goals also requires a willingness to grow. Growth must be controlled.

Many people feel that doubling or tripling a firm
overnight is the way this is accomplished. This is simply
not possible. It is a gradual process through improving the
company and increasing the experiences, acquiring more
qualified personnel and additional technical knowledge.
There are many ways in which management can improve
its ability to anticipate the requirements that growth will
entail.

Management consultants can show you many sophisticated formulas for projecting your company's growth,
but this is quite involved and costly. Designers can often
come up with a very simple formula themselves by match-
ing the needs of the prospective clients that they expect to
service and their design firm's qualifications and background. By reviewing the needs of the client and just what
the firm is able to do for the client, a profitable direction
can be established.

INCREASED PROFIT

There are two primary ways of increasing profit:
1. Increase the total sales or the amount of income
   secured by the design firm.
2. Increase the percentage of profit on all items that
   are expected by the firm. It is most important not
   to just simply grow in additional sales, but to
   carefully and and constantly review the percentage of profit on each particular job. This is a part
   of marketing as much as it is of any other financial program. In reviewing your firm's marketing
   program, you will want to carefully analyze the
   areas which are most profitable. Use this as a

guideline for creating marketing structure. A marketing structure must be based on work to be done, rather than work that has been done in the past. Be sure to use each and every staff member to his maximum ability. You may have to replace certain staff members in order to expedite certain projects.

It is interesting how many designers have learned to take a single project and capitalize on it. It may have been a small project, now because of his additional experience, has made him take a second look and reinterpret it so that it becomes a far more important and profitable one. During the last few years, I have seen examples of designers cutting the volume of jobs they are doing and highly increasing the percentage of profit. Designers must be careful to review the percentage of profits in the overall markup structure of your design work to be sure it is coordinated with your business objective.

SOURCES FOR MARKETING PROGRAMS

Interprofessionals. Engineers, architects, other professionals in our field are excellent sources for marketing. They often have jobs that may need interior designers.

Contractors. Both general and sub should be interviewed to find out what type of projects they are working on and whether there are any opportunities for the design professional.

Manufacturers, representatives, wholesalers, suppliers, distributors. All of these people have sales people out in the field and many of them are aware of future projects. This is an excellent source for the interior designer to develop.

Government. There are distinct types of people in government who should be interviewed. They are the contracting officer, the project officer and the department head. After defining the particular kind of government project, it is important to speak with the most knowledgeable person in that field in determining future outlines of government projects.

Government Officials. Often, the officials within the community are aware of new building projects. They are aware of new industries that are coming into a community. Association or rapport with community leaders is an excellent source for the designer.

Owners. Owners of any large project, apartment building, office building, are an excellent source of acquiring knowledge of new tenants. Normally they, as owners, are interested in maintaining a good standard within their building. This is an excellent source for the designer in acquiring new clients.

All marketing is guesswork. However, the more information that can be acquired, the more scientific and the more profitable it becomes.

THE FIRM'S EXPERIENCE

Analyze the firm's experience. It is necessary to review each of the activities and projects for the past five to ten years. Projects that were performed more than ten years ago will have little relevance to today's market unless for some reason they were particularly outstanding. But their usefulness in marketing today is somewhat limited.

Identify each project that the design firm has done during the last five years, the amount of work that was

involved and the type of project. An outline sheet is
included to give you some guide as to the information that
is necessary.

DESIGN STAFF QUESTIONNAIRE

NAME   DATE

EDUCATION

Design School or College   Courses Studied   From   To

Degree Received

Awards

Other Education - Workshops, Seminars, Etc.
Subject   Dates Attended

Employment Experience

Date   From   To
Company
Your Title
Job Description

Date   From   To
Company
Your Title
Job Description

Design Project Experience   Date
Type
Client or Owner
Cost of Total Project
Cost of Work Done by Design Firm
Services Rendered by Design Firm

40

Your Responsibilities

Accomplishments on this Project

Professional organizations which you belong to and offices or committees or posts that you have held in this organization.

Special abilities which you possess that you feel would be of benefit to the firm; such as certain social acquaintances, foreign languages, knowledge within other disciplines, list of prospective clients with which you are familiar or have had experience.

This survey sheet should be taken of all staff employees and kept in a file with the total biographical questionnaire. It should be updated on an annual basis so that if you are considering a new project, it can be very easily reviewed and perhaps certain information may help you realize the abilities of your firm when attempting to apply for a new client project.

THE DESIGN PROJECT ANALYSIS FORM

DATE STARTED

COMPLETED

1. The name of the project
2. The name of the client
3. The location of the project
4. The type of construction (new, existing, remodeling)
5. The size of the project
6. The amount of
    a. Construction budget
    b. Furniture budget
7. The type of services the firm provides

8. Design accomplishments
9. The profit on the project
10. The percentage of profit on the total project
11. The source of the job
12. Expected referrals

DEFINITION OF CATEGORIES

1. *Name of the Project.* The name of the project should be the one that you usually refer to: as to the particular name of the building or the name of the corporation, or the name of the residential client.
2. *Name of the Client.* The name of the client is the name of the person you have worked with or that you worked under on this particular job, whether it is a board of directors or whether it was the owner or a managing director of a project.
3. *Location of the Project.* City, same town in which you are located, or whether it is a distance from you. (Any information involved as to difficulties in reaching the project or other involvements as to communication problems.)
4. *Type of Construction (New, Existing, Remodeling).* Define whether it is new construction or remodeling and what other things are involved in this particular project: whether you as the interior designer were involved in part of the architectural planning or whether you came into the project at a later date where you were merely responsible for the furnishings.
5. *Size of the Project.* Break this down as far as you think necessary. Depending upon the size of the design firm, you may want to go further into defining areas of carpeting, wall surface materials, drapery and window coverings, down to art work, etc.

6. *Size of the Fee.* The size of the fee and the method charged, whether you charge an hourly rate, a percentage; actually, how you were paid for this project, whether you were paid through someone or whether you were paid as an independent designer.

7. *Type of Services the Firm Provides.* Outline the complete service, whether you did the basic design and followed through with construction inspections and feasibility studies, on through to the types of drawings presented and the complete synopsis of all services provided.

8. *Design Accomplishments.* The objective of the job, was this accomplished from the owner's viewpoint as well as the interior design firm's view? Is this a project which you are pleased to have on your list of accomplishments? Does it entail both the negative and the positive aspect of the job?

9. *Profit on the Project.* The net amount involved. This is calculated by computing all the costs, the personnel time, the materials, all products involved, if there were furnishings supplied and subtracting them from the overall income from the project.

10. *Percentage of Profit on the Total Project.* The percentage of profit on the total project is the net profit divided by the total contract value for your services. After you have made up a sheet like this for each of our projects, file or organize them into a yearly file so that you are able to judge how many projects you had undertaken during this particular year, what type of projects they were and how successful they were.

11. *Source of the Job.* It is important to identify the source of the job so that additional marketing information can evolve. Under this category, list the components that you feel contributed to the job; whether it was a

referral from an individual based on a previous project, or whatever type of references such as advertising, newsletters or any other media that you think might be involved. List all sources that you feel contribute.

12. *Expected Referrals.* After completing each job, review it from a future marketing viewpoint to see just how this job can be used to secure future projects. There are a number of ways that this can be done:

a. Interviewing the client after completion and discussing with him other projects that might be within his company or within other areas of a similar project type.

This review can often bring immediate referrals for other projects or referrals can come much later. At this meeting, you may discuss with your client the possibility of publicity exposure; whether the client would enjoy or consider magazine or publication exposure. It is important to review his attitudes before going further in this issue. Also, the job might be considered for other competitions on a design basis.

SUMMARY

Annual Form
Type of jobs done
Number of jobs done
Amount of costs for each job
Percentage of Profit

This sheet will help you understand the trends of your company as well as the trends of the marketing area around you.

Planning

One of the most important parts of managing an interior design firm is being a good planner and understanding the importance of planning your overall business objectives. I take one week out a year to devote to the planning and goal-setting for next year. I hire the very best business consultants I can find, professionals from different orientations, to help me.

I deal first with where I want to see myself as a professional, with the people I am working with, then with the financial goals of the company. We map out very carefully the success and failures of the past year by reviewing the financial statements, both my personal as well as my company's. We also review the income tax planning. This is planned ahead so that we do not hit the end of the year and wonder what happened.

Review your estate plan. Be sure that you have established this, that this is not something the government or other people end up doing for you. You really want control of this area and it must be reviewed on an annual basis.

Your retirement plan also requires thought and must be part of this planning program. We know as professionals that we must plan for our retirement from the beginning, the time we start working.

Plan your other investments. We need investments outside of our company, and they too should be reviewed on an annual basis.

Have an analysis done of your investment portfolio. Be sure your investment consultant is handling this in the way that you want it handled. Reestablish with him your goals and objectives for the next year. Set up a budget for your company. Be sure that you know where the money is going over the next year.

Determine which jobs have been profitable for you during the last five years and establish your marketing objectives. Then determine whether the staff that you have now is properly oriented to handle your objectives. Of your past jobs, which jobs can help you to acquire the jobs that you want to do over the next five years?

Determine whether you should get larger or smaller or stay the same. Determine which will be the most profitable direction for your company to go.

Determine whether you want to do jobs for glory or for money. Both are available, but very often they are not the same projects.

Review your problems of the past few years. Determine how you can eliminate as many of these as possible during the oncoming years.

Keep a list of what you consider as goals, objectives, problems, and items that you feel require general managing. As well best you are able, think of the outcomes if

46

these are handled in different ways.

Remember, all planning is based on assumption. This is why, within your planning, you bring together the best possible people that you can find and you establish a planning program based on their experiences as well as your past experiences, and chances are these assumptions can become realities because they have direction and planning.

As designers, we realize that it is important to plan and to create a master schedule for whatever our objectives are. We understand this completely in our design work, and this is a necessary component in our total business structure. We can decide that we would like to change or that we have exhausted the potential of what we are involved in or we just cannot emotionally tolerate what we are involved in. Don't make a change without establishing a direction and without testing that direction. Strategy is a crucial part of successful business development.

In order to plan my company's goals, I bring together some of the most outstanding planning personalities I can find. It is most helpful to work with someone who is in the interior design or a related field. They can often expose us to some of the marketing objectives of the field as well as the different trends that they have been exposed to.

Planning personalities are often different types of people than your accountant or your attorney. They are people that have more creative ability and more foresight within the business planning area. After the plan has been created, it is then time to review it with your accountant and your attorney to be sure that from a tax viewpoint as well as a legal and general administrative structure, it fits with your company's structure.

Planning for the year is not something that is done within an hour or so. It requires preparation as well as effort in study. It also requires trying out and testing. You just don't stop one business plan and begin another without first testing it to see whether your goals can be accomplished.

During the testing period, I often find that some of the best master plans and some of the strongest strategies can prove unproductive. I am forced, as we are often within our design programs, to restructure to reestablish our business goals. Planning and having an objective keeps me from being bored with the routine work load.

Find someone you feel shares your business objectives. It is almost necessary to go outside of your company, at least for your basic plan strategy or its review. Your company structure can be strong, but you do need a certain amount of outside direction within this area.

SELLING YOUR BUSINESS

To get the best price for your firm you must design your business structure to be taken over, and you must plan for the sale at least five years in advance. An established firm has acquired valuable clients, credit, good will and sources throughout the years and can be a great asset to the person or designer who acquires it.

The following things are important to consider before selling your business:

1. The financial statement. Very often small companies and closely held corporations tend to use conservative accounting procedures to minimize taxes. Inventories may be understated; salaries or fringe benefits may erode earnings. When you are thinking about selling, you should consider that the sale will be based not only on net assets but

also on net earnings. Begin this bookkeeping system just as soon as you realize that you want to sell your business. Three to five years ahead is preferable. Even if you have to explain this very heavy increase and change in your statement, at least the new buyer will understand what you are doing and what is the real potential volume for this company.

2. Structure the management of your company for continuity. If the firms lacks a well-managed base, buyers could not be interested. This is one reason an interior designer might acquire another firm: they see a good management structure that could continue with new designers.

3. Be sure that your business continues to keep up with the potential market. Be sure that you have not left your marketing back in a prior period. Continue to market for new business. Work on sales and develop your company for maximum earnings to the very end.

YOUR RETIREMENT PLAN

Many designers are self-employed or employed by a firm that does not cover us with a regular retirement plan. There are a number of ways today that we can acquire retirement plans but it is something that we must start planning for early in our careers. Two very popular retirement plans today are the Keogh Plan and the Individual Retirement Accounts or IRA.

The Keogh Plan. The self-employed, including owners of businesses that are sole proprietorships can use the Keogh Plan. The plan must cover employees and you must make contributions for them on the same formula that you use for the owner. Up to 15% of your net self-employed income can be set aside and deducted. Your year's contribution cannot be more then $7,500 for each individual.

IRA is for employees who are not covered by a pension or profit sharing plan. These employees are eligible to set up an IRA. The maximum annual contribution is $1500 or in some situations, $1750, but it cannot be more than 15% of your gross compensation.

The Keogh Plan and IRA are designed for employment income only. They cannot be used for interest dividend or other investment income.

Law permits the money from these two plans to be invested in four different ways.

1. With banks and savings and loan associations. Usually it is to buy a year's certificate or to set up a trust account and have the bank invest in other things for a fee.
2. Mutual funds.
3. Annuity or Endowment Contracts — These contracts sometimes include life insurance and this is permitted for the Keogh Plan but not the IRA. The portion paid for the insurance is not tax deductible.
4. U.S. Government Retirement Bonds.

The money from these plans can be switched from one investment to another usually without penalty and there is no tax on these earnings until the money is taken out after retirement.

It is suggested that you establish your IRA or your Keogh Plan early in the year and put money into these accounts as early as you can in the year rather than wait until the end of the year because all the money that is being accumulated applies to your account on a tax-free basis. So, do not wait until the end of the year to pay in your installments.

There are many institutions handling these retirement plans and it is wise to shop around a bit and see who is offering the best situation.

Marketing

There are as many approaches to marketing and salesmanship as there are types of people and areas.

Whether you market or not is definitely a personal matter and a business objective. You may not need this; you may have enough clients to supply you with all the income you require. According to magazine source surveys, most designers do need some form of marketing in order to enjoy the quality of clients you want.

Marketing, sometimes called distribution, is the performance of business activities connected with the movement of goods and services from producers to consumers or other users. In addition to analyzing these activities, marketing involves understanding the consumer circumstances and attitudes that determine the character of a major part of marketing activities; the business organizations that perform these activities; and relevant aspects of government regulations. In marketing the ability to recognize early trends is fully as important as knowledge of the current state of affairs.

Selling is the personal, oral presentation of products or services to prospective customers for the purpose of making sales. In the United States, it has become a highly developed technique based on psychological analysis and psychological application. The well-schooled salesman today bases his presentation on his understanding of the customer's buying motivations as related to the particular product. By subtle stimulation and manipulation of these motivations the customer is led to want to buy the product. The salesman ideally does more than make the customer desire the product; he tries to win the customer's regard for the company which sells the product (and) tries to extend the confidence and regard of the customer to himself.

MARKETING RESEARCH
FOR THE DESIGN FIRM

The purpose of marketing research is to identify additional marketing areas that are available to the firm in which the designer has potential interest and to evaluate the ways which might be effective in securing this business. The effectiveness of basic marketing research is largely in proportion to the time and effort that are put into it. The designer can hire someone to do all or part of this work for him. Very few interior design firms are large enough to afford this luxury. If you can, a directory of marketing firms that might be of use is the Bradford's Directory of Marketing Research Agencies, 50 Argyle Avenue, New Rochelle, New York, 10804. This directory

54

lists firms, their principal number of employees and describes the type of marketing research work that they do.

Study several tools of marketing research before selecting those you may want to use. Specific books or articles may concern themselves with matters effective in the entire marketing. The designer will be able to establish a market research plan by identifying the research objectives. Then determine how each tool could have impact. In many cases, they will overlap.

PUBLICATIONS

U.S. Government Publications. The U.S. Government is the largest publisher in the world. Much market research can be done from the materials available from the government, if you know where to look. The book that will help is "Government Publications and Their Use." It is available from Brookings Institute, Washington, D.C., 20003. Another is the popular guide to the U.S. Publications. Write to the U.S. Superintendent of Documents, U.S. Government Printing Office, Washington, D.C. 20402, and request catalogs and specific recommendations for publications, or contact the Small Business Administration Office or Department of Commerce Field Office.

Reporting Services. McGraw Hill publishes the Dodge Reports, available for each specific geographic area. This is an excellent outline of the buildings under construction within a given area, the firms that are designing them, the details of the contracts and other professionals involved in the projects.

Standard & Poor's Industrial Surveys. This is also an analysis of trends in construction, utilities, retails, transportation.

General Business Publications. It is important for the interior designer to be aware of general economic trends, and the specific developments planned by different organizations for which design services could be required. Publications that are helpful are:

1. The Wall Street Journal
2. Barron's
3. Business Week
4. National Business
5. Forbes
6. Time
7. The New York Times
8. The National Observer

Other local papers published by statewide business organizations can also be valuable, such as Business Magazine, Banking Magazine and magazines related to each individual discipline in which the interior designer is working. Newspapers and magazines should not be underestimated as they are a medium to which our clients are constantly exposed.

IDENTIFYING YOUR CLIENTELE

Before embarking on any marketing or advertising program, identify the kind of person you want to attract as your potential client. For example, if your focus is on hospitals, it would be foolish for you to allocate research funds or marketing energy in the residential area.

Consider the ability of the client to pay for the projects and services rendered. Designers are often so anxious to get a job that they do not do enough credit research. I have seen interior designers fail, not because of their own ability, but because they have taken on what they consider to be an excellent client who simply does not come through with the financial requirements of the job.

CREDIT REPORTING AGENCIES

There are many good credit reporting agencies available, the most common of which are your *local credit organizations*. This is your best source when investigating residential ciients. The *banking institutions* are also an excellent source. Your local banker, when approached, will often give you the details required.

If you have a business account, *Dun and Bradstreet* is probably the best source of business credit information. There are also local companies specializing in certain areas of professional or business enterprises. The cost of a credit check is probably one of the best investments a designer can make. I would also suggest that in addition to checking a person's credit, you attempt to find out several companies or sources that they have worked with in the past and interview them as to the type of client you will be dealing with and just how they handle their professional associations.

GEOGRAPHIC LIMITATIONS

After defining the design firm's abilities, select the area in which it is practical to work.

The locations of jobs can be critical to the outcome of the project. Investigate carefully the expediting requirements, whether in the individual design or as far as delivering the project. Residential projects which require an exceptional amount of detail, especially if they are a smaller project, must be done in a convenient locale. Otherwise, they become exceptionally expensive. If you are talking about larger projects, budgets, or expenses, perhaps additional mileage and travel is still within the range of possibility on these projects. As designers specialize in one particular area, they find themselves traveling throughout the world and with very practical results.

SOCIAL CHARACTERISTICS

Interior design is a refined art, used by a sophisticated population. Interior designers not only cater to the avant-garde, but also handle some of today's social problems. We have interior designers specializing in mental health areas, in social service problems, penal institutions, community centers, homes for the aged, and many others (which are listed on our list of organizations using interior design services). A well-trained interior designer is aware that he is prepared to serve all types of clients. The critical questions are: "Is the client interested and desiring the services?" and "Are they willing and able to pay you for your services?"

INCOME LEVEL

As prices are increasing, the income level for the average residential client is also increasing. In most parts of the eastern states, the average interior design client for residential work is earning $75,000 a year or more. People who earn less than that put most of their income into regular living expenses. However, there are projects other than residential which take in all income levels. Many interior designers specialize in some of these lower-income projects for the challenge and excitement. We see modular homes and many items being designed on the production line which were once limited to only the higher-income group. Designers are contributing much expertise in mass-produced items helping establish higher quality design within some of the lower-income levels.

DEMOGRAPHICS

The success of an interior design practice can be the result of the population and the economic development of the area in which the designer establishes residence. Take a look at the projected growth development of an area before establishing your firm. It is natural that fast-growing areas offer more design possibilities. Many interior designers operate from obscure locations. They have developed their particular specialities to a degree that make them in demand almost anywhere.

COMMUNITY AFFAIRS

Taking part in community affairs is an excellent way to show your future clients you are interested in their lifestyle, that you not just approve but you are a part of it. Many designers have acquired their total client list by being active in community affairs. It is important, however, to choose something and to be active in something in which you are really interested.

Watch your position on controversial issues. As a general rule, it is not good marketing to take sides. Some people and are very active in political and highly controversial social issues.

I think one must consider one's source of clients when analyzing a desirable type of social service work to be involved in.

MARKETING TECHNIQUES

REFERRALS

Referrals are probably the best source for new clients. Since design is a sizeable investment, future clients really want to know something about you. How can they find a better way than through referrals?

Clients with whom you have previously worked are

probably your single best referral source. They know how you work. They know how you handle a job. This is, therefore, a key area for securing new clients.

Friends are also a valuable referral source. Since it is essential that the designer understand the personal lifestyle of clients, your friends could be an excellent source of future clients. Some people can work well with their friends—some people prefer an arm's-length relationship. You alone must determine whether friends are a good reference, but this is how many designers started their careers.

Architects, engineering firms, or *other professionals* in related fields are also a good referral source. Real estate brokers are an excellent source and one where many designers have obtained all of their referrals. A good relationship with professionals in other fields can be an excellent medium for securing future new clients.

HOW TO PROMOTE THE DESIGNER

The Budget. The figure generally budgeted for promotion is 3 to 5% of gross income (not gross sales), although some consultants suggest 5 to 10%. I suggest you put this amount of money aside specifically for promotion (to be sure that you have future jobs). New businesses may need more than this—you may go to 10%. This should be a predetermined amount, something that you plan to advance, not something that just happens after the year ending.

Your Business Card. One of the first things that each of your clients will see is your business or calling card. This should include some of the very basic standards of all business cards: regular in size; name and title; telephone and area code; address and zip code; company name; what you do; logo (if you have established one). All of these items should be included on your calling card. To eliminate any one of these may cause great problems at a later date because you have no way of knowing into whose hands this card is going to fall. The business or calling card is your insurance that you are represented properly when you or your staff cannot be there in person. Great care should be taken to make sure it is correct. *NOTE:* It is important to use someone who is qualified in graphic design for both your stationery and your business card.

Your personal appearance is part of your calling card. People may make judgments as to whether or not they will retain you as a professional designer merely because of your personal appearance. The standards of your personal style are obviously created to correlate with the type of clients for whom you will be working.

Stationery should be of a standard quality and a color that will take erasures and a type of correction fluid. Use reasonably well-designed stationery and business cards; the two are best when they co-ordinate.

Letter of Interest. Sales letters are an important medium for everyone. Since you now have stationery, these letters are an inexpensive way of directing your particular business to the attention of good prospective clients. Your letter should:

1. Suggest that you understand the client's problem. Identify that the client to whom you are writing had a problem, and that you understand it.
2. State your standard practice of working.
3. Set a date for a follow-up. Follow up on the letter. There is no point in sending out sales letters if you do not properly follow up on them.

Brochures. A brochure can be done very simply or very expensively. Simple folders or brochures are a very good form of advertising, and they can be something that you can read with your client. The brochure could have a plain side on which notes can be written when discussing a particular issue with a client.

Whether your brochure is expensive or inexpensive is not the main factor. It is important that it be well designed. You might want to use a graphic designer on this project. The brochure should state what an interior designer is—what you do—and perhaps provide some form of question and answer. The key here is good design (and be sure it is current) stating something that will be of appeal to your prospective client.

Use care in distribution; mass marketing usually produces less than a 3% return. Like your portfolio, your brochure should be reviewed as the nature of your business changes at least every two years.

Whether you are a beginning designer or a polished designer, *your portfolio* is an important part of your professional presentation and must be updated constantly. This does not mean that some of your older designs cannot be included but you must have it in readiness at all times and it must be reasonably representative of your work. Initially, it might be the portfolio you created in art school. As you progress, it will include jobs that you consider complimentary to your design talents. Your portfolio or design presentation may be slide shows, photographs, brochures, etc. Your style and presentation of your portfolio will vary according to the particular area of design in which you are working. Your presentation should be adapted to your client's needs. Therefore, a portfolio that can be varied according to requirements is most desirable.

I recommend that you use *professional photographers* who are familiar with interior design work. These special photographers are available in most areas and their costs vary according to the locale. Be sure to consider the final use of your photographs in determining whether you need transparencies, black and white, or color shots. One reason for photographs is for your own reference, but they can be most effectively used in public relations work.

If you are planning to use your photographs for any form of PR or marketing project, it is advisable to check with the publication in which you hope to be published to find out their particular requirements and standards on photographic form. Don't invest in a form of photography that that particular publication cannot use.

You might try to get your client to agree to pay half of your photography fee. Clients may be interested in having these photographs for many reasons: pride, prosperity, security, insurance, or, if it is a business or professional account, they might enjoy using these photographs as part of their marketing or PR program.

Creativity in photography is exceptionally important. If you are using a photograph for a magazine or publication, be sure it is a properly laid-out and well-designed photograph. Magazines want something that is attractive. Even if you are forced to move furniture or alter your design, be adaptable when working with the photographer in order to create a proper composition in photography form.

Entertaining expenses are deductible when the goal of the evening is to acquire a sale or is directed for definite, clear business services. You do not need to get the job in order to take the tax deduction, but you must prove you are working toward a job.

Entertaining in your home can have many great advantages, especially for interior designers. I know many designers who entertain quite frequently. It is not enough just to simply entertain; you must define the objective.

Entertaining really has many advantages. Very often you and your guests feel more at ease. It is a chance for your family to interact into some of your business situations. It is much less expensive than a restaurant and far more creative and unusual. Be sure that your food is something that is planned individually and is not something that is simply catered as everyone is doing.

For a profit-oriented evening, keep your party down to approximately eight, no more than 10 people. If it gets to be too large, you will not have the opportunity to interact with your clients.

Some designers entertain in a client's space before beginning a project. Other designers have gained permission to give a party in completed client space. I think this could prove to be quite profitable and if your clients would permit this, this can be a great advantage. Use your creativity in entertaining but document what you spend so that you have no problems with IRS. Estimates are no longer accepted. You must have receipts and your program for the evening must be clearly defined.

Show houses give you an opportunity to present your talents. It is good exposure for the many people who are interested in the design world or in retaining a good designer. Show houses have many different regulations, which should be investigated before going into the project. You should also check on the responsibility of the coordinators of the show house and be sure that you, as a designer, are being treated fairly. In some areas you are permitted to staff the rooms. If you can, you have the opportunity of meeting prospective clients. Many houses today do not permit you to be present during the show. Since show houses are expensive, this could be a detriment in using this method of advertising. If you elect this method it is something you ought to do well in order to properly represent your design talent.

In metropolitan areas many of our wholesale sources will supply designers with their products to use in their show house displays. This will reduce the cost of doing the show house considerably. The staff that is planning the show house will have a list available of sources that are willing to supply things such as paint, carpeting, furnishings, electrical fixtures, as well as many services such as paperhanging, carpentry, etc. This list should be made available to you when you are negotiating your room within the show house. In small towns, this is often not possible and this makes the cost of doing show houses considerably more expensive.

Many designers *donate their services* to charitable organizations. I think it is important to submit a bill for one principal reason—to let the client realize the value of the services that you are donating. Very often, designers will donate their efforts to a church or to other community organizations and put many, many hours or weeks into a project, and the client feels that they are getting something that took no effort or was of no financial value. So that you receive proper recognition, do see that they get a bill and perhaps even a quotation ahead. It should say, in effect, this is a project I will do for you, the cost will be so many thousand of dollars and I am willing to donate this as my contribution to the project.

As far as taxes are concerned, this invoice has no value. If you take $1,000 and donate it immediately to charity, it cancels out as income on which you would pay federal tax. You would not be able to use it as any substantial deduction. If you do run it through your books, you may have to pay state and local taxes, as well as social security if you are self-employed.

If you have a corporation, you are only permitted to donate 5% of your income per year for charity. This can carry over to another year, but you must be careful not to show over 5%. And, you will have to pay taxes on the money that you have donated. Any items that you give to a charity is deductible at the designer's cost, not at list, and you must have invoices to support this.

PUBLIC RELATIONS

Public relations has three purposes:
1. To make you known to your resources.
2. To make you known to your peers.
3. To make you known to potential clients.

One of the easiest, least expensive public relations devices a designer can do is to enter the contests sponsored by design resources. Very often, you are competing with fewer people than you are on the average design bid. Most contests want actual installations as opposed to conceptual drawings. You may have to rephotograph or to write up the jobs so the description answers the contest requirements. Even if you do not win, your work has been exposed to magazine and newspaper editors and may be published.

Is it worthwhile to hire a professional publicist? Yes, if you can afford to support a long-term campaign. Most editors plan a week to nine months in advance, and people rarely act immediately on what they read. They may carry a clipping around for years before they can afford to hire a desinger. Public relations is an investment in time as well as money. Don't hire a professional publicist unless you have something to say and work that is as good as the work you have seen already published.

Publicity can only introduce you to the public. Your ideas, your work, and your professional demeanor will sell a reader on whether he wishes to contact you.

Before considering hiring a public relations person to develop your career, it is important to understand that it requires a considerable budget and a portion of your time for the planning and development of this PR program. It is normally best to allow a budget for about a three-year program. A review each six months is suggested to determine whether the goals and objectives of your PR person are line with your marketing program.

In order to have a successful PR program, one must have a definite marketing objective and find a professional PR person who is willing to develop this for you. PR programs are normally successful when the designer has a positive long view toward this project and is willing to support the PR person with everything necessary to make their program successful. We cannot expect a PR person to do the job alone. It requires time and energy on the part of the designer.

When selecting a PR person, investigate the field you want to market and find someone who has experience within that field. Select someone you want to to make part of your team, someone whom you enjoy working with. One of the most difficult parts of PR is attempting to find the right areas and the right places in which to place the different articles and promotion that might be valuable to you. It is very difficult for a PR person without the right background to do a job successfully.

How To Charge

Many interior designers charge a straight hourly rate. Other charge a percentage on the item purchased, or on a percentage of the cost of the total purchases. Some discount the retail; others add to it. There are so many equations for how to charge that it is almost impossible to give anyone a guideline without reviewing his own requirements and expenses.

My formula is to outline the budget for the next year to determine exactly what it costs to run the company per year. When I know the per employee cost and the general production, I have my accountant review it. He comes up with an overall budget and suggested mark-up procedure.

Earlier in my career I thought the only professional way to work was on an hourly basis. At that time some designers earned a living by working for furniture stores and getting a percentage of sales. I was told that being a

69

professional and selling furniture were poles apart. Now I see the reverse. Many designers say there is no possible way to maintain the expenses of their firms on just an hourly fee. They must go beyond that and earn a percentage of the items contracted for.

Hourly rates in the interior design field range between $25 and $200, and some designers in large cities earn still more. I find that interior designers very often cannot successfully charge more than do psychiatrists in their cities. I do not know why this is.

As you consider each job, look at it in terms of the benefits you can expect to accrue from it. Balance your financial expectations and the amount of time you expect to put into it, and consider the marketing value of the job. We have all done jobs that were not overly profitable, but brought us several jobs which were.

Your client should be made aware of the way you charge and the way you handle finances. Asking for a *retainer or a deposit* is important; it is part of the professional contract. In several states, designers have been discouraged from using the term "deposit," because legally a deposit requires that you maintain a separate escrow account for that client and do not mix the funds with those of other projects. In New York State, this almost became law, and I believe several states are considering it. It is safer to call the money a retainer.

I charge a design fee or a retainer on every project. The minimum fee is $1,000. I really cannot do a design study for less, and larger projects require larger fees. I review this with the client during the initial interview and the design fee is payable in advance.

After one of my seminars on design professionalism, a woman confided that a number of her fellow designers had criticized her for not charging a design fee. "Really,

I've never done it and I don't think my clients would be comfortable with it." She worked out of her house from 10.00 a.m. to 3:00 p.m. She did $120,000 in business each year—$60,000 gross profit—and the clients paid all freight and delivery expenses. She had a part-time secretary and low overhead—about $3,000 annually for telephone, postage, supplies. Her husband paid the rent.

Anyway you looked at it, she had to be making between $40 and $50 thousand a year, which is rather good for five hours of work a day. Her method worked for her. If you are not satisfied with your firm's earnings at year end, perhaps you should review some techniques to improve your profits.

Last year, our accountant brought to our attention that the cost of merchandise had increased 11% in one year's period. We had been used to very few increases on price of merchandise and had always given our clients a firm quotation on all merchandise they were purchasing from us. We found that we had quoted under our normal mark-up procedures, but that our cost of merchandise and the delivery increased 11%. This, with some additional increases in our office and overhead expenses, caused us to lose money because in our firm we attempt to get between 5% and 10% net profit on our annual gross income. With an 11% increase, we obviously lost money. As you are aware when we buy things, it is not at the price listed on the price list, but at the prices the item is on the day the item is shipped to us. This can vary considerably from the amount estimated. We must very carefully watch this when we quote jobs. When we expect something to cost $4,600, we allow approximately 10% variance. We would quote $4,600 to $5,200, so that in case we have an increase, we have some cushion for it.

Although you are in some cases selling products, you

only have one real thing to sell and that is your time. Be sure you are properly compensated for each and every hour of time that you spend. If you take on a large design project and you are selling items, be sure there is enough profit there to make the project worth your while. It is still a matter of time equals money.

Traveling Expenses. Many of us are working in more than one location. When evaluating whether you should take the job, do consider the cost of traveling expenses, in gas and wear and tear on your car, as well as hours. This must be included in the costs of expediting your job. It is possible to spend so much time traveling that there is no way that to make a profit on the project. Travel expenses are something IRS is watching very carefully, so document your expenses. For anything over $25.00, you must have a receipt. The use of your company car must be defined. Is it used totally for business use or partially for business? This makes a difference in the amount you are allowed to deduct.

We keep a simple *cost sheet* on every project. It need not be elaborate and could even be done on the back of your work order, but there is no way you will learn how to estimate future projects if you don't evaluate expenses now. You may have learned how to estimate in school and relearned as a young professional, but the skill becomes more sure with practice.

In many cases the difference between profit and loss lies in one's *ability to sell*. The word sell has acquired a derogatory sense, but I feel that if you are a professional in any field, you must be able to promote your services. If your gross income is the same as last year's, but it costs more to run the firm, you need additional business to compensate for inflation. You might find it in sales. Do you know what you need to produce each week, each month?

72

The time it takes to expedite a job is another factor in profit and loss. The sooner a job is out of your office, the more profit you earn and the shorter time your money is tied up. Every dollar you hold now costs you a minimum of 1½% to 2% a month to handle.

SALES VS. PROFIT

I have reviewed the profit problems of several companies. Very often interior designers do not do enough business. In the past, interior designers could do $100-$150,000 worth of business in the retail field and be making a moderate amount of money. In the contract field, a large company did 3 to 5 million dollars a year. Today in the contract field, you are no longer one of the big one hundred. To be considered a large design firm, we must be doing much more business. However, in working as a consultant, I have suggested that some firms *reduce* their sales and be more concerned with how much profit they are earning on each job rather than having a lot of sales.

A company that has done over five million dollars worth of business each year for the last five years has lost money every one of those five years. There are so many situations like this within the interior design and contracting fields. Job costs must be noted on each job as a necessary reference for any form of estimating.

Twenty years ago, some designers made money on financing a job. Bank interest rates just passed 20%. In Pennsylvania, we may legally charge clients only 18%. I am better off letting the bank finance them. I simply don't have that large an amount of capital, and what I have I prefer to use for other purposes.

Outline your cash expectations with your clients. Are

they aware that money costs money? When I am working on retainer, I explain to the client that using their money to finance the project is less expensive than using mine. Most clients are happy to provide the cash required.

Most of the breakdowns in incoming cash flow occur because of lack of communication and poor handling during the project. If you have made your client aware of your financial expectations, if you have worked each aspect of the job to completion, is you have kept your client properly informed, you should have no problems at the end of the job and the final payment.

A few minutes of research at the start of a project have proven valuable to our firm. When we begin a project, we check the credit expectations of the client. We see if they have enough money for the retainer, and whether they have the money to complete the project. If they do not, we will arrange credit for them with one of our banks. The time we spend here saves us much aggravation at the end of the job.

Interior design can be a profitable business. Review your firm on a quarterly or semi-annual basis to see what it costs and what profit it generates. In the past, once a year was adequate. With rapidly changing costs, it should be done more often.

BILLING RATE FOR DESIGNER
— $24,000 per year salary

The billing rate for a designer at $24,000 a year is calculated on the base salary of $24,000, figuring approximately 50 weeks would be $480.00 per week and there are 30 billable hours in a week which would give you a cost rate of $16.00. And, $16.00 cost times a calculation of 2½ times equals $40.00 per hour. Times three would give you $48.00 per hour. Normally, if someone is getting $24,000 a

74

year, you would bill them out from $40.00 to $48.00 per hour.

COMPANY COST RATE FOR DESIGNERS —
$24,000 per year salary

Direct labor	$24,000
Fringe benefits	7,200
Total cost per person	31,200
Divided by 50 weeks per year, which would be	$624.00 per week

If you work 40 hours a week, we can only calculate 30 chargeable hours and so 30 divided into $624.00 would equal approximately $21.00 per hour.

PERSONNEL COSTS

Salary	100%
Holidays - 10 days	4%
Sick Leave	1.5%
Vacation	4.5%
Unemployment Taxes	2%
F.I.C.A.	6.13%
Workman's Compensation	2.67%
Insurance - Medical	6%
Group Life	1.7%
Pension Plan	
	128.5%

Average billable hours   80%

30% of $24,000.00 = $7,200.00.

ACCOUNTS RECEIVABLE

The proper collection of accounts receivable can be the single most successful or failure issue within an interior design firm. Handling money and the time it takes to turn over the money in a project can mean the difference between profit and loss.

Many companies who have great design jobs are forced into bankruptcy because they have not handled their accounts receivable properly. In several sad situations designers have been forced out of business and into bankruptcy because they were unable to collect their accounts receivable—in many instances, for reasons that were not necessarily neglect within the interior design firm. Even under the best circumstances, it is difficult to maintain the proper cash flow.

To expedite and handle accounts receivable, you must:

Review and analyze your client's ability to pay for the job before taking it. It is crucial to review this with the client; determine exactly what the cost of the job will be and what their position is in handling this expenditure. In developing a job, projects grow and the initial budget is not enough to cover it. Clients expect a job to cost perhaps $30,000, find that with the additions they have made, it may end up costing $45,000 or $50,000. The cash is in the client's company account to handle a $25,000 expenditure, but some financing must be arranged for the additional amount.

Before beginning the job, I review the client's financial responsibility. If the cash is not available, I will try to get it for them through our sources if they do not have a source available.

Address your *remittance expectations*. Clients often feel it is fine to pay an invoice in 90 days or 120 days. They are used to doing this with other suppliers who extend them credit as their way of creating a loyalty with their products. If an interior designer expects to be paid faster than the 90-120 day period, he should say so before beginning a job.

Some clients are lax in paying even though they are a good credit risk. Before you begin a job, explain what retainers you require. The normal policy in the interior design field was one-third at one time, but many firms today require a 50% retainer. Many designers also ask for payments as merchandise is received in the warehouse or in-progress payments. Firms in larger cities will send a billing prior to the day of delivery with a note saying "We are going to deliver the furnishings for your facility next Thursday. Enclosed is an invoice for $65,000 for the furnishings we will be installing. We shall appreciate having your check available on the day of delivery." In smaller towns, this would not be considered proper business courtesy. I think it does depend upon your client and upon your circumstances. The important thing is to explain this ahead of time.

Send out your bills immediately after installation. Many designers tend to be lax in sending out bills. This is a mistake. When something has been used or worn and the client has had it awhile, it is not as appealing to pay for it. It is important to see that the billing goes with delivery or immediately the day after delivery. If your firm seems businesslike, you will find you get much faster payment. If you are lax, the clients may get the idea you do not need the money.

Cash Discount. You may be able to bring in their accounts receivable at a faster rate by allowing a 1% or 2% cash discount for rapid payment. It can decrease the amount of costs in both money you borrow to cover accounts receivables, as well as bookkeeping and expediting costs. It may be well worth the 1% or 2% to be sure that you are turning over your accounts receivable at a fast rate.

Cash discounts have been considered the thing of the past, but I think we are going to see many more of them.

We run a credit report on each and every business and personal account we work with. We think it is important to understand the client's manner of payment so that we can be sure that it adapts to our expectations.

Check your bookkeeping department and be sure your invoices are going out regularly. Many design firms discover that invoices go out weeks to months after the order has been delivered. It really must go out right away. Do not accept excuses from your bookkeeping department.

Determine how quickly all your orders can be processed and shipped. Tightening this lead time can boost your cash flow.

Require a monthly report from your bookkeeper outlining exactly all accounts and what position they are in. Be sure that the designer or the client coordinator is aware of exactly how these accounts stand.

Insist on accuracy. Any billings that go out to a client should be thoroughly checked to assure that there are no mistakes. If a client finds errors on the billing, they question the whole costing procedure.

Our bookkeeping system for accounts receivable is a simple one-write system which has saved us an immeasurable amount of time.

EXPLANATION OF THE
ACCOUNTS RECEIVABLE LEDGER CARD

This ledger card, which is part of a one-write system, has worked very well for us, especially in handling the deposits. We normally receive a sizeable deposit on a job, and it is important that it be credited to the various merchandise shipped as designated. By picking up one card at any time, we can tell exactly when the client has paid, just what is owing us, as well as how the deposit stands.

1 2 3 4 5 6 7 8 9 10 11 12 13 14 15 16 17 18 19 20 21 22 23 24 25 26 27 28 29 30 31

NAME **KEYSTONE ASSOCIATES, INC.**
ADDRESS **123 OAK LANE**

BALANCE FORWARD → **476 68**

DATE	FOLIO	DETAIL	A	B	C DEBIT	D CREDIT	E BAL.	F DEBIT	CREDIT	BALANCE
10-18-79	18-37	WALL COVER						1354 04		1830 72
11-7-79	19-3	CARPET						2573 42		4404 14
11-12-79	20-12	PAID							1830 72	2573 42
12-3-79	19-27	SOFA, CHRS.						1349 60		3923 02
12-16-79	21-6	PAID							2573 42	1349 60
12-20-79	20-5	CONF. TBL.						750 49		2100 09

(CHARGES — DEPOSITS)

ACCOUNTS RECEIVABLE LEDGER

Top Table

DATE	DETAIL	DEBIT	CREDIT	BAL.	DEBIT	CREDIT	BAL. PAID	BALANCE	NAME	TAXABLE	COLLECTED	RETURN	NON-TAX	RETURN	NON-TAX BAL PAID
BALANCE FORWARD		3,100 00								15,129 65	816 94	-0-	1,474 95	-0-	390 60
1-10-80	24-1 CNDL. ABRA			133 03	183 03		1	-0-	TIMMERMAN, ROBT.	125 50	7 53				1
1-13-80	24-2 GBR. CHR. & SPREAD			2329 92	892 84		2	2 497 08	ROMANO	839 27	53 57				2
1-16-80	24-3 WALLCOVER			1481 00	517 28		3	913 72	KEYSTONE INS. CO.	488 00	29 28				3
1-17-80	24-4 DRAPE. & WALLCOVER			4603 31	3987 61		4	505 70	HAMN, A.B.	3,748 35	289 26				4
1-20-80	25-5 CARPET			3071 46	3071 46		5	-0-	ALCORN SERVICES INC.	2,887 17	184 29				5
1-20-80	25-6 ARM & GIAS CONS		500 00	4785 30	1038 80		6	3 746 50	BARTLEY ASSOC.	980 00	58 80				6
	LESS DEPOSIT			4285 30		500 00	7	4 785 30							7
							8								8
							9								9
							10								10
							11								11
							12								12
							13								13
							14								14
							15								15

Bottom Table — CASH RECEIPT SUMMARY / CHARGE SUMMARY

DATE	FOLIO	DETAIL	MISC.	INTEREST INCOME	A/C REC. DEBIT	CHARGES DEBIT	DEPOSITS CREDIT	BAL.	A/C REC. DEBIT	A/C DEC. CREDIT	BALANCE	PREVIOUS BALANCE	NAME	AMT. REC'D	BANK TRANSIT NO.	DEPOSITS AMOUNT
BALANCE FORWARD				325 17			5190 00		15,532 81			2,104 98				
1-18-80	17-1	PAID CK# 595							1000 00	868 35	1	1868 35	TIERNI, J.W.	1000 00		1
1-19-80	17-2	PAID CK# 650							186 97	-0-	2	186 97	CRONENBERG	186 97		2
1-19-80	17-3	PAID CK# 624							341 00	2676 46	3	3016 46	AJAX INC.	341 00		3
1-19-80	17-4	PAID CK# 580							206 70	-0-	4	206 70	ENGLE, A.B.	206 70	1-19-80	1734.67 / 4
1-21-80	17-5	PAID CK# 426							1300 00	5793 38	5	7093 38	PRESSLY ASSOC.	1300 00		5
1-24-80	17-6	PAID CK# 3593							19 08	-0-	6	19 08	POTTS, L.C.	19 08	1-24-80	1319.08 / 6
1-26-80	17-7	PAID CK#							2158 93	733 16	7	2892 09	ROMANO, M.A.	2158 93		7
1-27-80	17-8	PAID CK# 4402							605 37	-0-	8	605 37	SLADE, W.E.	605 37	1-27-80	2764.30 / 8

CR — CR — CR — E — A/c DEC. CREDIT — A/c REC. DEBIT — DR.

☐ CASH RECEIPT SUMMARY   ☐ CHARGE SUMMARY

Letter of Agreement and Contracts

In order to avoid misunderstanding during a job as well as unpleasant financial risks, use a letter of agreement. This letter specifies exactly what services the designer will complete and the conditions of the services, and it serves as the formal acceptance for the services by the client.

There are many types of letters of agreement and contracts available. ASID recommends a version of the AIA's standard form of agreement for the interior design services, designed in 1977.[1] This is an extensive contract

---

[1] The American Society of Interior Designers has two standard contract forms: a Contract for Professional Services, stipulated sum; and a Contract for Professional Services, hourly rate.

suitable for very large jobs, but many parts of this contract could be adapted to smaller projects.

The AIA also has a general condition contract for furniture, furnishings and equipment; a contract document involving details from the architects, owners, contractors, through to the termination of the contract.[2] This very formalized agreement can also be adapted for small projects or used in its full form.

Your letter of agreement should include:

1. *A description of the project* stating the areas to be involved, the location of the building, the type of services the designer is going to render. If the client's project is different from your expectations, it is better to learn it at this point than further along in the project.

2. *Your fee and appropriate budget estimates.*

3. Just what *services are to be performed* within these areas: Are you doing just a color consultation, a floor plan, or are you detailing the final expediting documents and providing purchasing specifications? It is imperative to outline just how far the services go for the amount of fee that has been established.

4. *The dollar amount of the retainer.* It is customary to receive a retainer at the outset of a project. Establish how it is to be handled: is it a retainer against a study fee, or is it applicable to the future contract and furnishings?

5. *The methods of payment.* This section states what

[2] The American Institute of Architects offers a Standard Form of Agreement for interior design services, and a separate agreement entitled General Conditions of the Contract for Furniture, Furnishings and Equipment.

84

is due when the contract is received, how much is due when the design is presented, and what percentage is due at installation.

6. *Purchasing details.* If at this point you know whether the designer or the client will do the purchasing, spell out the conditions and schedules accordingly.

7. *A description of method for establishing fees.* If a set fee is established for the design concept, you may want to limit the number of hours. Spell out in detail exactly what is included within this fee.

8. *An explanation of responsibility* between designer and other sources such as workroom, other crafts people, furniture sources, etc. How responsible are you for the quality of work supplied by your sources? How are you compensated for designing, planning and specifying the requirements for the other sources?

9. *Add-on services.* It is important to outline just how this would be handled with the client so that the client is not constantly adding on projects that have not been reviewed in the original requirement statement.

10. *Other financial details* such as freight charges, state or local taxes that might be involved in the contract.

11. *The client's responsibility* as far as preparation of the job or any materials that the client must supply the designer such as existing blue prints or specifications from other specialists on the project.

12. *Your compensation.* An outline of just what the client's responsibilities are as far as your compensation and method of payment is clearly outlined

so that the client is aware of exactly what he is responsible for and when payments are due. It is crucial to establish this in advance so that he understands what obligations he will have in thirty days, sixty days, etc.

13. Outline any *other conditions* you feel might affect the job such as the completion of other crafts people or certain construction details that may alter the completion date of your design or project.

Establishing Credit
and Accounts Payable

CREDIT

Handling money is an essential part of any business. The interior design business depends a great deal upon the ability to handle considerable sums. We need a good established relationship with a strong banking institution. It is much more difficult to establish credit than it was five years ago. Money is extremely expensive and banks are not looking to make loans.

The best way of acquiring a working relationship with the banking institution is to make that bank part of your business. Banks are interested in companies when they know the function and purpose of the business and a great deal more.

Make that banker and banking institution a part of

your company and you will find that he will be far more interested in you than one might expect and will help you in acquiring ways of financing your business today.

When you make the initial contact, give your banker the type of information he needs to make a proper evaluation of your firm.

The following is a check list of the information that your banker will need:

1. The type of ownership of your firm: corporation, partnership, or individual.
2. Product or type of service you render.
3. Competition in your area.
4. Market available to you.
5. Your sales and service facilities, including any special and unusual services you provide to your customers.
6. Your employees: How many, their qualifications and what they contribute to the company;
7. Your financial administration: Who is your CPA and what is your general business administration structure?
8. Your present financial statement.
9. A history of your financial background.
10. Any outstanding loans.
11. A list of the companies you have worked for and the jobs you have done for them; the dates and approximate size of the jobs.
12. A list of your sources.
13. A list of the clients you have worked for.
14. A list of any banks or lending institutions you have worked with in the past.
15. The goals and objective of your company. Carefully review these with your banker and update them on a semi-annual basis.

Although borrowing today is more difficult than it was in the past, there still is some money available from various sources. If your situation is presented properly, your chances for securing the money are much greater and usually if you have met the following requirements, the money will be available to you. Before you approach the bank, review your financial needs with financial advisers within your company, and such outside professionals as your CPA. You need to show that whatever money is borrowed will be used for a good profit, and you need to be able to provide the required collateral. Your accountant and financial manager can help supply this kind of information.

Attitudes toward borrowing vary. Since mine is conservative, I am often sorry that I have not taken more of a risk.

A banker will want specific information when you are negotiating a loan. I suggest you keep a summary of these points available:

1. The size of the loan required.
2. The purpose of the loan.
3. When the funds will be needed.
4. The collateral available to secure the loan.
5. How the loan will be repaid.
6. The cash flow forecast covering the period of the loan prepared by your accountant.
7. Personal credit data of the owner or partners or associates of the business.
8. Any life insurance that can be available as collateral for the loan.
9. Any outstanding loans you may have.
10. A history of your business.
11. Your financial statement for this year and for the three to five previous years.

12. Some evidence of your reputation for paying your obligations.

A line of credit. The banker extends a line of credit and makes an advance commitment that he is willing to loan the designer money under certain conditions. This is often done on a revolving basis. Designers usually find this type of financing advantageous because it is adaptable to particular jobs that they are working on. Since it is on a short-term basis, it can be more easily controlled according to the design projects.

Term loans. Short-term loans normally cover less than a year, sometimes only thirty to sixty days. A term loan is usually desirable because even though the interest may be higher it is for a short period. In most cases it can be paid off in advance if the project is completed and the monies are available sooner.

Arranging loans for clients. At initial presentations with clients, I have found that many of them are not financially prepared to handle the total project. Some have estimated $20,000 for a project that ended up with a cost proposal of $35,000. They may find it to their advantage to go ahead with the project but haven't the cash available at the moment. In order to clarify their arrangement for payment and make certain that my money will be available when the project is completed, I like to review with them their payment plan. If a client does not have financing available, I have arrangements with several banking institutions to which I can go, with the proposed project along with some information about the client's financial background to arrange the loan. Because of the size of the loans, they are usually made directly to the client. I am not involved nor in any way liable for their responsibilities. This can be important for designers and should be carefully considered with each project because it assists their

90

cash flow tremendously if the monies are available at the completion of a project.

Although money is expensive, in many cases it still pays to borrow in certain situations. With inflation, the project next year will cost us at least 10% to 20% more. Since the client has the use of the project during this time period, very often it pays them to do it *now*. We must be careful when borrowing to be more concerned about the length of the borrowing period and how we are using it, since it is now costing us such a high percentage of interest. So, borrow when profitable, but with more care than ever before.

KEEPING A GOOD CREDIT RATING

Keeping a good credit record is probably one of the most important things an interior design firm can do. Designers can easily become dependent on suppliers with whom they have credit, to the extent that they pay excessive prices and sometimes even compromise on quality. Designers can ruin their practices by not maintaining a good credit standing.

File regular reports with Dun & Bradstreet and Lyon's or similar credit reporting services. If your firm is new, you should file on a semi-annual basis. After you have been established ten years or longer, probably an annual basis is sufficient.

Have your accountant send them a financial statement just as soon as it is prepared. Also, give the credit rating organizations a list or summary of your next year's expectations so that they will be well prepared to give accurate information on your company.

If you are having difficulty and find that you require

more time to pay certain invoices, let your creditors know that you are going to take this additional time. Keeping them well informed exactly what you are doing and why is the best method of maintaining good credit.

I have worked with a number of companies who have been in a situation of bankruptcy or near bankrupcty. In some instances, it is possible to get creditors to work with you. One of the first things we do in a situation like this is to make a complete history of the financial status of the company and the projected format. Send this with an existing financial statement to Dun & Bradstreet and Lyons as well as the leading creditors with which you have issue at the time. Explain to them your situation, how you intend to cover the particular bills that are stated. Very often, they will attempt to work with you. They see you as a future account and they want that account. If they do not know what you are doing, they are just as frightened as you would be if an account is not paying you. Be sure that your creditors know your situation. Update credit reports on a regular basis; also see that your larger accounts are kept abreast of your credit.

You should also maintain a regular credit reporting system with your bank. Then, anytime you need additional credit, their checking process is shortened.

Check regularly with Lyons and Dun & Bradstreet to learn how you are rated and why, and remember one of the easiest ways to get a bad credit rating is by not keeping these agencies informed. The following are the addresses of Dun & Bradstreet and Lyons:

Dun & Bradstreet, Inc.
99 Church Street
New York, New York

Lyon Furniture Mercantile Agency
315 Fifth Avenue
New York, New York 10016

ACCOUNTS PAYABLE

The companies that we deal with must maintain a cash flow just as we must. To maintain a good relationship with the companies you purchase from, establish a standard procedure for paying bills within your company. This may mean that you pay your bills twice a month, once a week, within ten days of receipt of invoice, or within thirty days of receipt of invoice.

When you find a new line you would like to use, you should establish credit with that company before placing the first purchase order. In our company, we require that credit be established with each and every company that is put on our catalog shelf. We do not want to place an order only to find that it will take another sixty or ninety days for a credit review before the firm will consider opening our account. This only delays projects and causes difficulty in expediting the job.

If you keep your companies informed, you will find that they will work with you in most instances. Each company with which you have established credit should be aware of your bill-paying procedure. It also helps to let them know of any delays or any alterations in the way you pay your bills. Most difficulties arise when designers have not established a procedure. Other financial problems may mean they are not able to keep payments up to date. The companies hear nothing from them and therefore assume the designers are in very difficult financial straits.

In our company, we think it is important to see that invoices are handled and paid as quickly as possible. Our policy requires the managing director pay bills within ten days of receipt of merchandise. We will not pay any invoice until the merchandise is received and inspected. Each invoice that arrives is marked with the date we received it, the date we received the merchandise, the date of inspection, the signature of the person who inspected it.

Many of our sources do not like the smaller designer accounts because they are much more difficult to manage than store accounts. If you keep your accounts payable up to date and the manufacturer is aware that you pay promptly, it makes your company a far more desirable accoiunt. Very often it will mean that you will get merchandise before someone else.

This a record of the liabilities that a firm owes for materials, equipment, wages, rent and utilities, taxes and any loans or notes that may be payable. There are many ways of setting up an accounts payable system. In our company, we attempt to do this as simply as possible, with a one-write check disbursement system. The one-write system permits us when writing a check to immediately write into our accounts payable disbursement journal the amount of the invoice paid and then by simply extending them on the ledger page, we can automatically know just what the expenses have been incurred for. This saves a tremendous amount of time per week. Since we write approximately 700 checks per month, we find that this saves approximately two days in office staff time by using this system.

We have a regular day per week that this is done so that all checks are written at one time except for small checks that come in daily which are regular occurrences. Those are written immediately upon receipt.

If you maintain a simple system and take care of your accounts payable immediately, you can find that you will save a tremendous amount of time in handling invoices and reviewing different issues. Also, by paying currently, you may take advantage of many cash discounts.

Maintaining good credit can be one of the greatest assets a design firm can have. If you are a small firm and you always pay your bills promptly, you will find that

94

many companies will be happy to serve you. You will also find that very often you will get merchandise ahead of others because your sources know they can expect fast turn-over on their money.

CASH DISCOUNT

A number of companies still offer cash discounts. It is amazing how much an interior design firm can earn per year just on the 2% or 5% discounts which are allowed them by certain companies. Many of our carpet manufacturers allow us 5% discount if the invoice is paid within 30 days. Balance due 60 days which means that for just a 30-day period, we are losing a 5% discount. It has paid us to borrow money in order to be sure that we gain this 5% discount.

By taking discounts, we can also keep ourselves in an excellent credit position.

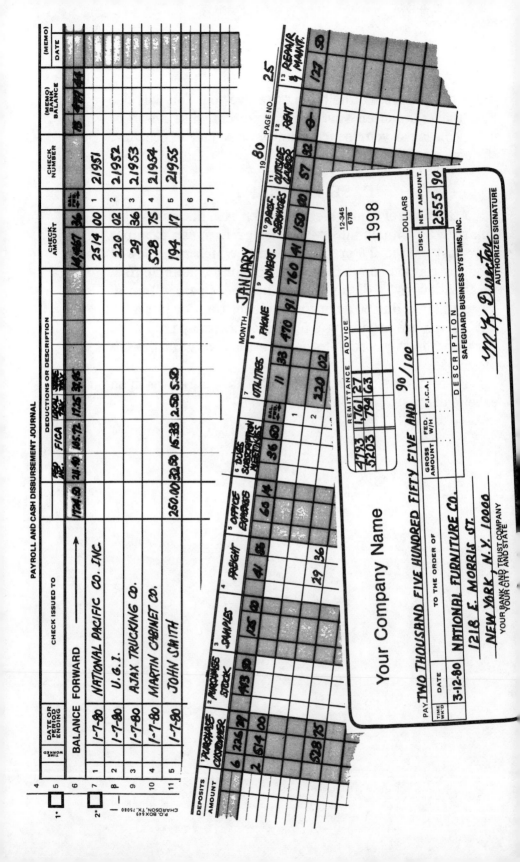

Business Consultants

YOUR ACCOUNTANT

You need the services of an accountant from the time you begin planning your office throughout your practice until you sell it. Too often, accountants are treated as post-mortem people. to get *maximum value*, we must *learn to use accountants in our planning* stages as well as for our annual review.

Invite your accountant to look over *all* your future business plans. If he becomes part of your company, you will get more from the relationship. Have your accountant review your leases, loan agreements, contracts and any long-term commitments before you are inextricably involved. You may want him to review your insurance and perhaps comment on the policies you have purchased. Because the accountant knows your financial needs, he is able to spot quickly whether the coverage is in the right amounts and what else you should have. This can be exceptionally helpful. Have him review your business plans. Subtle flaws can have unbelievable tax consequences or can greatly affect your cash flow.

The more your accountant knows about your operation by invitation and the less he has to discover by searching and probing, the more valuable he can be to your firm. He is paid by the hour, so it pays you to make his job easy. I recommend inviting your accountant and your attorney to regular meetings where you and they discuss the advancement and structure of your company. Be sure they know each other and are familiar with what each other is doing on your behalf.

Meet with your accountant no less than two to four times a year and pick his brains in every aspect of the financial parts of your business. It is important that he understand more about your business than just the financial aspects.

When it is time for your accountant to take your books, be sure you have all the up-to-date records and all the numbers ready. If you want the lowest accounting prices possible, use your own bookkeeping staff to prepare the records. It is difficult and expensive for an outside person to come in and up-date your records. Have them ready for him, on time, and in clean, readable condition, and you won't be paying accountant's prices for clerical work.

Don't be afraid to ask your accountant questions but remember that he is conservative. This is his orientation. If you have stated a plan of action and he suggests this is not financially feasible, or he does not recommend this, don't be afraid to ask for alternatives. It may be only one phase of the project that is inappropriate. You can easily adjust your plans.

You should understand every form and report he gives you. If you don't understand it, ask him to explain it to you. If he doesn't explain it so you understand it, find someone who can explain it to you in terms you do understand.

Learn to talk with accountant. Use him often and explain to him what *you* would like to be done and how *you* would like to do it. Say to him, "This is what I would like to accomplish and how can we do it?", start him thinking as to how it can be accomplished from a financial viewpoint.

Our accountant here has worked with me since 1956. Mr. Samuel Ledger became our accountant because he was very easy for me to understand. He taught the CPA's locally and was used to explaining things in elementary language. Every time I am considering an addition, a subtraction, opening another business, closing one, or whether a move or change is economical, Mr. Ledger is one of the first people called in. There have been times when I had projects I thought were extremely exciting that I would love to do and he has shown me how it is really not profitable. The taxes and additional accounting records that would be required make some plans impracticable.

Before I met Mr. Ledger, I worked with a firm that had many accountants who insisted on doing it "their way," who really didn't care what the company wanted, only that it was done according to accounting principles. These accountants felt that they were superior because of their accounting backgrounds but they could not communicate with the company principals. I think it was most important to me starting to have someone who was able to relate to me in terms I understood. The first accounting Mr. Ledger did for me was my annual taxes. I would take him my little red book every year and he would do my accounting and charge me $25.00 a year. The account has grown considerably and he has taken on a number of other accounts that we referred. He has become part of our company over the twenty some years and I think he has learned to enjoy us as we have learned to enjoy him.

YOUR ATTORNEY

You need an attorney during the organizing period of your business to determine the form it will take. Should it be a sole proprietorship, a partnership, a limited partnership or a corporation? There are other types but these are the most usual ones. I suggest you, your attorney, and your accountant work together to tailor your business structure.

We use attorneys in contract interpretation, contract drafting, contract review, and in working out problems with clients who file suits. Negotiating with employees and drawing up employee contracts are other situations where an attorney might be used.

Maintaining your business structure can also be in your attorney's domain. He might assist in preparing corporate minutes, corporate resolutions, and in the documents required for tax and legal purposes.

In determining an effective business structure for you, the first question your attorney needs answered is where your money comes from. Is it borrowed from a bank or financial institution, or are there other arrangements? Is it from a single source or from a group of people? What form does the capital take? And, finally, who else is involved in the business?

It is important for you to outline your goals at this point, and to establish just how active a role you expect your attorney to play in the future of your business. Acquaint the attorney with the details concerning your business.

Do you have a business in a different field? You will not wish to jeopardize its success.

What particular problems do you foresee?

What is the purpose of the business?

What is its location?

What registrations will you need?

What stock will you issue and to whom?

I asked a number of attorneys how large a part should an attorney play in a company structure. In essence, "as large a part as the client requires" was the answer. Some people emotionally need someone to bounce ideas off. An attorney is a good person for this, but an expensive one. Other people only talk to an attorney when they have a definite problem—a lawsuit or a contract dispute, for instance.

I think there is a middle ground. For an attorney to give you the best service, you should bring him in before the final die is cast so he can mold the manner in which the issue is handled. Consult with an attorney if you think there is going to be a suit; don't wait until someone sues you. The attorney can help with the negotiations or preparations for a possible legal suit.

Selecting an attorney is difficult. I think the best way to go about it is to compare notes with another business. Ask for recommendations from people who have used an attorney's services. It is important to deal with an attorney who is interested in and handles small businesses. Some do not want small business accounts.

You can find an attorney by consulting recognized law listings. Probably the best known directory is the *Martindale-Hubbell Legal Directory,* available in most public libraries. It lists attorneys by representative clients and gives financial references. It also rates the lawyer for general ability and overall reputation.

The Martindale-Hubbell has three categories—A, B, and C—for general ability. To be eligible for any of these categories the lawyer must be in practice for a particular period of time, and must be rated by fellow attorneys. While "A" is the highest rating, many good attorneys do not have an "A" rating simply because they have not been in practice long enough.

In general, reputation rating "V" stands for very high. An attorney with an "AV" rating is well above average in ability, but a person with a "BV" rating may be just as good.

When you meet with the attorney you have chosen, discuss your business objectives and your interests. Attorneys are not necessarily enthusiastic about everything presented to them. From experience, they know that everything that crosses their desks is not necessarily going to succeed. But we hire lawyers for their skills and experience, not to have the same enthusiasms we have.

The lawyer will try to diminish your enthusiasm to see if you have both feet on the ground and that you are aware of the realities. It is part of his orientation.

The question *you* should ask is whether the attorney will do the work himself or farm it out to another lawyer. Very few lawyers today practice in a one-person office; most are in partnership or are part of a large company. If you expect your attorney to do all the work, make it clear at the outset; he will price accordingly. You should have some idea from him who will perform the legal services and how it will be handled, so that you are not disappointed with the outcome.

Judging the quality of an attorney's work can be just as difficult as selecting the attorney in the first place.

Results are the best guide here. Does using this attorney reduce or eliminate the number of disputes and litigations for you? Are you in trouble with tax authorities and other aras where he represents you?

Are letters of agreement really binding? Do we really need contracts like the AIA/ASID contract or is there another more valid form? Several attorneys have said that there is no contract written that guarantees against dispute and misunderstanding. However, contracts are valuable because they spell out some of the areas of possible dispute and litigation. They define and make the client aware of potential problems. They acquaint clients with trade terms and familiarize them with the ways interior designers charge and calculate their fees. So, I feel a contract is valuable in clarifying your communications and diminishing misunderstanding.

It is not necessary to use a contract, but if you choose not to and something happens, you are the person who did not take the initiative and time to clarify to your client your position and services. Therefore, not to use a contract could be asking for trouble.

What kind of records should a designer keep to support him in the case of a lawsuit? My lawyer said that if you kept extremely complete records of the sort he really likes, you would probably get nothing else done. It is practical to keep a record of all business transactions, copies of all purchase orders and requisitions.

While a job is going on, keep all the correspondence with suppliers and anything written to your client. If you do run into trouble, at that point you should write a memorandum of each and every detail you recall about the job. Months later, one does not remember as well. Be sure that you keep the documents in an orderly file, and keep the file for six years unless you think the situation involves fraud, which is usually tax-related. Your accountant can also advise you what records to keep and how long to keep them.

There are many other legal issues designers should be aware of: state laws, federal laws, and city laws pertaining to the practice of design, for instance. An attorney can tell you about these, but a better source is perhaps trade or professional associations. Very often things are brought to my attention by the American Society of Interior Designers or by the Chamber of Commerce. I later discuss these with my attorney to see how much importance I should attach to them.

Insist on good rapport between your attorney and your accountant. It is crucial that they work together on your behalf, that they understand what the other is doing —or there may be needless duplication in their work.

YOUR INSURANCE PROGRAM

Your insurance agent or broker is an important part of your financial advisory group and should work with your accountant and your attorney. Select someone who will be available to you at all times, and who is compatible with the rest of the group. This working rapport is just as important as his ability and the knowledge he will offer you.

How do you select an insurance agent? Again, it is important to find someone you can work with. Another businessman or one of the financial professionals in your advisory group might help you select a competent and capable professional.

Do you want an agent or broker? An insurance agent normally represents one insurance company. A broker will represent a number of companies and can negotiate to determine where you can get the best coverage and the best prices on that coverage. In most instances, you are better off today with a broker or a person who is both an agent and a broker. The combined agent/broker has great strength and rapport with one or several companies but has other lines available to you so that he can handle your whole package. He is the middle man between you and the insurance market, and earns a commission in handling your insurance programs. Unless the insurance agent understands the interior design field, it is very hard for him to define your needs. The reason for his talking with your accountant and your attorney is that they will outline what insurance program is required for the particular needs of your company.

BUILDING PROPERTY

Property coverage insures against many of the components that involve risks to your buildings and premises. Very often a company will write a package policy that is less espensive. The package works best when it is designed for your particular needs, rather than just a regular pre-packaged policy. You will probably need insurance in some of the following areas:

Fire Insurance is one of the most important considerations in the interior design business. You must have an adequate appraisal of the replacement value of the building to determine the proper amount of insurance required. *If* the co-insurance clause is attached, be sure insufficient insurance will not penalize the insured in the event of a loss.

Building and Contents applies to the described structures and the permanent fixtures belonging to and constituting a part of the building. Machinery used in the building service, such as air-conditioning systems, boilers, and elevators, constitutes parts of the building covered under this policy. Location of the building very often will alter the rate of this particular policy.

Replacement Costs Endorsement provides for the full reimbursement of the actual costs of repair or replacement of the insured building without any deduction for depreciation.

Extended Coverage Endorsement covers your property for the same amount as your fire policy against all direct loss or damage caused by windstorm, hail, explosion, riot and civil commotion, aircraft, vehicle and smoke.

Vandalism and Malicious Mischief. Endorsements on your policy to cover the loss and damages caused by vandalism and malicious mischief.

Flood Insurance protects the owner of dwellings against financial loss in catastrophic floods including inundation from mud slides. Flood insurance is written in areas declared eligible by the federal government and coverage can be obtained through your local broker through the National Flood Insurance Program. The cost of this policy is partially covered by the federal government. It is very economical at this point.

Contents and Personal Property. Insurance is carried on all furniture and fixture and inventory. General coverage is similar to the building property.

BUSINESS OPERATIONS

Accounts Receivable Policy protects the insured against loss related to the inability to collect accounts receivable when books and records have been destroyed, lost or damaged.

Valuable Papers coverage covers the loss or destruction of valuable papers such as mortgages, records, finan-

106

cial data, product specifications, merchandise records, customer lists, blueprints and plans and specifications that might be used.

The Transportation Floater provides an all-risk coverage for the designer's property while in transit, either while being delivered to the customer or while en route from the merchant from your source to the client.

A Bailees Customer Floater insures against the loss by fire, burglary, hold-up, and windstorms. Any articles or materials that the interior designer might have accepted from their client for renovation, repair or merely just working under general conditions. It covers the client's property while in the possession of the interior designer or craft people.

A Business Interruption policy reimburses the designer for the profits he would have earned if the fire or other hazard had not occurred. It includes reimbursement for continued expenses, including payroll for a specific number of time or days.

Earnings Insurance is a simplified earning business interruption policy. It is suitable for small businesses whose earnings are not regular and are difficult to forecast. This is based on a pre-determined expected profit amount.

General Liability Insurance. Interior designers and other professionals are subject to the threat of third-party claims. Injury exists as long as there is a client on the premises. It does not terminate when the doors are closed. The designer and the manufacturer are often named jointly in suits allegedly caused by injuries due to defective products. There are policies designed to cover the interior designer in most issues where protection is required against injury or property damage.

Comprehensive General Liability insures against all

declared existing hazards plus unknown hazards occurring during the policy term, that might come from the designer's offices or business operations. It is a good idea to have this policy written in conjunction with your automobile policy and your product liability policy, so that the company covering you will cover you as completely as possible.

Personal Injury is popularly called the "false arrest insurance." This coverage is often added as an endorsement to the general liability insurance policy. It insures against libel, slander or defamation of character which the designer or an employee might be accused of due to an attempt to protect their property.

Medical Payments policy pays up to a certain amount, with specified limits on customers and other members of the public injured on the premises as a result of the insured business operations.

Workmen's Compensation insures any employee, due to the statutory liability resulting from personal injury or death suffered in the course of their employment provided under the workmen's compensation law. Workmen's compensation is mandatory in most states and has varying minimums depending upon state requirements.

Motor Vehicle Insurance. Since many designers provide delivery service, you must insure the trucks and other delivery vehicles against damage or loss. The same is true of any passenger cars. It is most important to have high liability coverage for all vehicles used in the interest of business.

Automobile Liability insures against the loss or damage of the designer for reason of liability or body injury or provides property damage to members of the public for any operation of the business autos or delivery trucks.

Employers Non-ownership Liability covers your busi-

108

ness in situations where employees might be using their own cars for business purposes.

Hired Cars covers the use of any hired cars. Additional delivery trucks which are rented during business periods can also be included for a minimum premium under this policy.

Collision insures the designer against the loss of collision or upset of his motor vehicle in the use of his business.

Comprehensive Insurance insures the interior designer's business, automobiles and other motor vehicles against loss, fire or theft or other physical damage hazards including glass breakage.

Professional Liability Insurance is now available for interior designers which covers liability for claims resulting from the commission or omission of professional acts. Such claims are often without merit. Nevertheless, they are troublesome and expensive to defend and this policy guards against these possibilities. It is now available through ASID for interior designers.

Product Liability Insurance is designed to cover any liability regarding malfunctions for claims resulting from misuse or use of products installed by the interior designer.

Group Life Insurance may be purchased by businesses for the benefit of their employees. It may be written to provide minimal amount of insurance for each of their employees subject to increases as to the individual's period of employment lengthens. This may be made totally the company or partially by the employee.

Disability Insurance. There are great varieties of disability insurance plans which are available from both casualty insurance and life insurance companies. Most interior designers work on their own or with small firms, and should have good disability insurance. In my own situation, it proved very helpful and I recommend every designer have some policy to give them some form of income during any time they may be disabled due to illness.

Group Hospitalization Insurance provides coverage for hospital confinement benefits similar to those under Blue Cross-Blue Shield plans.

Major Medical pays medical expenses arising from illnesses and accidents up to a specified amount. These policies are often done in coordination with your group hospitalization.

Transportation Damage Insurance is a fairly new insurance which is really very valuable because under this plan, a designer does not need to file a claim with a carrier for merchandise damaged in transit. There is an additional charge of 2% added to the net invoice of any merchandise covered by this order which is damaged in transit and will be replaced at no charge or credit to your account as preferred. The company must have notification in writing of the exact nature of the damage within ten days of receipt of the merchandise. Damaged merchandise must be kept for inspection. This is an excellent insurance—especially for very breakable items such as lamps and many fragile accessories.

It is impossible for interior designers to carry all the insurance that they might like to have. It is important that your insurance advisor, your accountant and attorney, as well as your business advisor, give you some comment as to which are your greatest losses and which ones you can afford to cover and which you cannot. There are some coverages which may pay us to gamble on because we just cannot afford everything. But we must attempt to cover our business with the major ones because one very sad loss can destroy a business.

By taking higher deductibles on certain insurance policies and doing some self-insuring, small companies can save a tremendous amount of money. The advantages are that it reduces the premium and also does give us a tax advantage at the time of loss, if we should have a loss. The government shares in this risk by giving us a tax advantage.

Higher deductibles are advised on property insurance of all types, in bonding employees, and on automobile insurance; not on anything that involves liability insurance. The reason for not involving liability insurance is that this would cause a third-person claim, which can get very complicated in terms of legal settlement.

Look over all your insurance for the last five years. See which ones you normally do not have claims on. Check with your company to see if by raising the deductible on these policies from perhaps $200-$500.00 on insurance or from $1,000 to $10,000 on property insurance, you can save yourself a considerable amount of money.

INSURANCE CLAIMS

When we buy insurance, we hope we will not have to use it. If you do have to use it, these guidelines may help you in handling your claims with as little problem as possible.

Calculate your losses accurately. Many business people cannot determine the extent of their losses or theft because their accounting system and record-keeping procedures are not in order. Interior designers have a better opportunity than most professionals. At most times, we do know the cost of replacing or restoring whatever property loss we might have.

Present the claim properly. If we overstate, we automatically begin many questions and problems in settling the claim. Be careful not to understate; this is just as inaccurate as an overstatement.

Review your claim with your accountant and your insurance agent before presenting it to the adjustor. If it is not presented properly, you will not get the results you seek.

Be sure the coordination between your office and the insurance company is handled by one person. Have this person follow through carefully to be sure that there is a record of all details and that all interaction between you and the insurance company is documented for future reference.

As designers, we know what contractors we want to use in restoring a project or who the merchandise came from initially. So, present this to your insurance adjustor. Normally you will be able to use the person you want.

Use your insurance consultant or agent as one of your negotiating group. He has a very strong play with the insurance company since he is purchasing the insurance in your name. Let him take your stand. Be sure he is aware of each and every detail of the negotiation. This is an excellent opportunity to find out the value of an insurance agent. Just a few months after moving into our studio, we had a small fire.

On July 14, 1978, on a Friday afternoon at approximately 3:00 p.m., I was working with a client in my office and I noticed that there was smoke in the building. When I realized what was happening, I started looking through the building to see if I could find the source of the smoke.

After checking for approximately one-half to three-quarters of an hour and realizing that the smoke was not just my imagination, I called the fire department and asked to speak to the fire chief. I told him we had smoke in our building, and although we had looked very carefully

112

through the building, we found no noticeable sign of a fire. I asked if he would send someone who had more experience in finding sources of fire. I asked that he not send a truck or make any more commotion than necessary considering that this is a commercial building.

Within a few minutes he and a staff member were here. Within the next hour they found no source of fire but agreed that the building was full of smoke. Our installation man and I followed them through the building.

After another forty-five minutes, the fire chief called for a general alarm, because the building is a three-story brick structure. The general alarm brought hook and ladder trucks, approximately fourteen pieces of equipment, filling the whole block. By this time, it was close to five o'clock on a Friday afternoon, and the traffic was considerable. The attraction of fire trucks made a tremendous traffic jam on our corner.

The men proceeded through the building, and I *worked with them* the whole time. We finally decided that it could be in a crawl space between the third floor ceiling and our roof. I called the general contractor who had worked on the building and asked if the hatch on the top of the roof was still there.

He said, "Yes. Why do you want to know?"

"We think we have a fire."

So, he explained the roof construction to me and I relayed it to the firemen. Mr. Brown, our contractor, then called every major subcontractor that worked on the building: the electrician, air-conditioning and heating engineers, etc. They arrived within a few minutes and worked with the firemen in helping to locate the position of the fire. I accompanied them in each area. I was concerned but did not panic. I was afraid they would start cutting up the building.

By entering the roof from the exterior, the firemen located the fire in the crawl space in the north rear corner of the house. I went with the fire chief up to the room, looked up and noticed that one of the wall washers was beige instead of white.

"Gentlemen, there is the fire!" I said. The firemen moved all the furniture away, put a large tarp over the floor, and put a large tub in the center. The fire chief said, "Okay, now you can pour water." All the water was contained into the large tub and into the tarp. The area burned out was approximately a four foot square in the rafters above this downlight.

The cause of the fire was improper installation of insulation. This smothered the lighting fixtures, which then caught fire.

After the fire was carefully put out and the firemen left, the contractors made emergency repairs. The next problem was to get rid of the smoke. We had a local company, Disaster Masters, who were excellent in removing smoke and whom we had used in several other jobs. I called the company immediately and they said that they would be here within a half an hour and would work all night on the project. I then called our insurance agent (it was now 7:30-8:00 p.m.), and told him what had happened and that I had hired smoke removers. He said definitely go ahead to do anything that would prevent further damage in the building. They worked all weekend. By Monday morning, the smoke situation had been cleared beautifully, and we were back in business. The repairs were taken care of during the next week.

Because we were able to manage this fire and had every detail covered by someone who really knew how to handle it, we eliminated many, many thousands of dollars worth of damage to our new building and new furnishings. We also eliminated any problems of business interruption because we were back in business Monday morning.

Special Project Consultants

Using an outside consultant has many advantages. The consultant is someone you voluntarily bring in to work with your staff and your clients on a particular project. You selected this person because his talents and skills suit the needs of the project, and the project is his only responsibility. The relationship is also a temporary one.

The consultant can support you in selling a job or in dealing with intercompany problems. He can help you with work standards, and the responsibilities of maintaining a design firm. Often someone outside the firm can help reestablish the discipline that gets lost through a long, friendly relationship with staff and clients.

No matter why you hire a consultant, if you do not give him all the details and describe the problem in an honest and open fashion, he will not be able to give constructive assistance.

The typical consulting procedure is to:

Define the problem. He reviews with the client just what the client thinks the problem is.

Work on the problem with you. You create alternative plans of action that can be developed and tested on the project.

Train a successor. It is often necessary to train a staff person to take over that particular role when the consultant leaves.

Try out the solution. Usually you have a testing and action period. At this point the consultant will back out and let you carry on alone.

Assess and reevaluate. Consultants usually return for an assessment to see how the strategy can be polished.

Even if you have sought consulting services, it is important to talk with other people. Who have they used as consultants? What type of relationship developed? You might speak with your accountant or other designers to find a business consultant. If you have a lighting problem, a lighting manufacturer may know of lighting consultants.

With the increasing complexity and sophistication of interior design, almost every professional firm uses a consultant of one form or another on a weekly or monthly basis. If you do not have confidence in your consultant or you do not find the working relationship comfortable, you would be better off to find someone else.

I take one week out of the year to sit down and plan with a business consultant other than my accountant or attorney what I expect and want for my firm for the next year. This is an expensive process but I find it worthwhile. The decisions we make and the thinking patterns we develop influence what happens in the next year. Without this yearly reevaluation, I think it would be almost impossible to keep business and personal accomplishments headed toward our goals.

TEAM DESIGN

Today designers often work as members of teams composed of related and apparently unrelated disciplines. We not only collaborate with architects, but lighting and acoustical engineers, industrial designers, landscape architects, communication and computer technologists, behavioral scientists, etc.

Many of these disciplines have formed trade associations, which may help narrow your search when you need a particular specialist to add to your team. A list of design and design-related associations follows this chapter.

SUPERVISION

Supervision may become a part of the interior design profession in the next few years. It is part of the structure of several other professions, notably in psychology. After a psychologist earns his Ph.D., he selects as his supervisor someone who has been in the profession for a long time, whose work he respects and who will agree, for a fee, to supervise the younger professional's work by reviewing the cases together.

I envision the same thing for interior design. I would like to see a supervising system created, either through a professional association like the American Society of Interior Designers or within the education system, so that designers have access to a supervisor. It could work not just for the beginner, but for someone who is starting a new area of endeavor and wants active supervision and advice from a senior designer who is not competitive.

Department of Health, Education and Welfare	330 Independence Avenue SW, Washington, DC 20201
Department of Housing and Urban Development	451 Seventh Street SW, Washington, DC 20410
Department of the Interior, National Park Service	C Street Between 18th and 19th Streets NW, Washington, DC 20240
Department of State, Office of Foreign Building Operations	2201 C Street NW, Washington, DC 20520
Department of Transportation	400 Seventh Street SW, Washington, DC 20590
Environmental Protection Agency	401 M Street SW, Washington, DC 20460
National Bureau of Standards	Washington, DC 20234 (mailing address)
Office of Education	400 Maryland Avenue SW, Washington, DC 20202
Public Buildings Service, General Services Administration	Eighteenth and F Streets, NW, Washington, DC 20405
American Crafts Council	22 W. 55 St., New York, NY 10019
American Institute of Architects	1735 New York Ave. NW, Washington, DC 20006
American Institute of of Building Design	839 Mitten Rd., Ste 206 Burlingame, CA 94010

American Institute for Design and Drafting	3119 Price Rd., Bartlesville, OK 74003
American Institute for Graphic Arts	1059 Third Ave., New York, NY 10021
American Institute of Landscape Architects	6810 No. 2nd Place, Phoenix, AZ 85012
American Management Association	135 W. 50 St., New York, NY 10020
American Society of Interior Designers	730 Fifth Ave., New York, NY 10019
American Society for Quality Control	161 W. Wisconsin Ave., Milwaukee, WI 53203
American Standards Testing Bureau	40 Water St., New York, NY 10004
American Society for Testing and Materials	1916 Race St., Philadelphia, PA 19103
American Society of Landscape Architects	1750 Old Meadow Dr., McLean, VA 22101
Association of Women in Architecture	7440 University Dr., St. Louis, MO 63130
Business & Institutional Furniture Manufacturers Association	2335 Burton SE Grand Rapids, MI 49506
Color Marketing Group	1000 Vermont Ave., NW Washington, D.C. 20005
Construction Specifications Institute	1150 Seventeenth St., NW Washington, DC 20036
Graphic Artists Guild	30 E. 20 St., Rm 405 New York, NY 10003

Industrial Designers Society of America	1717 N St. NW Washington, DC 20036
IFI	Keizerspracht 321 Amsterdam, 1002 Netherlands
Institute of Business Designers	Merchandise Mart Chicago, IL 60654
International Association of Lighting Designers	40 E. 49th St., New York, NY 10017
International Society of Interior Designers	8113 W. Third St., Los Angeles, CA 90048
National Academy of Design	1083 Fifth Ave., New York, NY 10028
National Association of Furniture Manufacturers	8401 Connecticut Ave., Washington, DC 20015
National Home Fashions League	P.O. Box 58045 Dallas, TX 75258
National Committee for Effective Design Legislation	200 E. 42nd St., Suite 2700, New York, N.Y. 10017
National Council of Architectural Registration Boards	1735 New York Ave., Suite 700, Washington, D.C. 20006
National Institute for Architectural Education	20 W. 40th St., New York, NY 10018
National Safety Council	425 No. Michigan Ave., Chicago, IL 60611
Society of American Registered Architects	180 No. Michigan Ave., Suite 1710 Chicago, IL 60601
Textile Design Guild	30 E. 20th St., Rm 405, New York, NY 10003

Management

Interior designers are not trained to be managers. Many successful designers have little or no managerial ability. Yet, we are forced every day to assume this position, to take on the management responsibility of each and every job that we design. To be forced to manage small companies or corporations is another common assignment.

It is sad that design schools and firms do not interview to determine whether we have the abilities for management as well as the abilities to design.

I often talk to designers who, pleased with the growth of their firm, are prepared to hire additional employees. They go out looking for other interior designers with similar orientation, which I think is a very big mistake. The first person you hire should be one with managerial ability. It was pointed out to me a number of times, "Mary, do not hire someone with the same ability as yourself. Hire someone who likes to do things you do not enjoy. Don't hire a duplicate of yourself."

Workshops in management techniques are easily available. One of the very popular ones, and one I think is adaptable to the interior design field, is Management By Objectives. This means establishing your objectives and working toward them, then measuring against your final objectives. This technique works with small as well as large groups. So often firms go on without any goals or objectives. This particular management theory requires you to constantly define your objectives and then to evaluate everything according to them.

Leading a small firm can be more difficult than leading a large one. It may help to make the small group part of the team or partners. Talking about "our" firm, what "we" do, instead of what "I" do, helps in this teamwork approach.

Be very conscious of sharing the credit for successes on your jobs as well as pointing out mistakes. It is important to make the few in your team very aware of the total objective of a project. It helps them understand the reasons for some of your decisions.

If you give one of your staff authority, support him. It is unfair to put a person into a position of responsibility and then not give him the respect that is required.

If you make a committment you are not able to fill, explain the reasons for it.

Delegate to staff members responsibilities for different parts of the job; especially parts that they are capable of handling, but be careful not to forget what you have assigned them. Establish a checklist so you have constant reference for any managerial instructions you give.

Many interior designers are overstaffed and would be better off with fewer, more capable employees rather than the large quantity of incapable or weak ones. Hire the very best people that you can find. They are always the least expensive in the end.

Having a lot of employees does not necessarily achieve profitable objectives. Often firms are better off to require more production from the few employees that they have and to be able to pay them at a higher rate.

If you are responsible for the management of your company, study managerial techniques. Find a few that are really adaptable to your personality and use only those that are really comfortable for you.

If management is your responsibility, expose yourself to education and workshops. I found it helpful to talk with managers of other firms, of different disciplines. I have taken from their background and pulled ideas which are suitable in the managing of my own firm. I have learned more from my clients and from my business associates in other fields than anyone can begin to measure. Look at the way other people are working. Maybe you can learn something.

A good manager is one who has the ability to make people want to follow them voluntarily.

Some mistakes many managers make are to assume employees know exactly what is expected on a design project. They expect that they know just whether they are doing well or whether they are not. They do not often comment and give them a measurement of their successes or failures. Many staff people do not have any idea how to improve. They may want to, but they don't know how. "Practice does not make perfect, only perfect practice makes perfect." (Vince Lombardi)

The good manager spends between 80 and 90% of his time with staff and with people. If we are still going to continue to work as designers, this is almost impossible and this is why, as designers, we must decide whether we as designers should be the manager or whether we should hire a qualified business person.

HOW MUCH DO YOU COST?

Do you know how much you cost? Figure out exactly what you cost, what each of your employees costs and then determine whether each of you is really earning what you are being paid. A person's cost is not just the salary he takes home. It includes all of the fringe benefits: vacation, sick leave, extra time off, business lunches, the trips to conventions or shows, the car and all other expenses and benefits that you enjoy—such as extra travel and meetings and things that you are able to do on company expenses. You find that you are paying a lot of extras. Health insurance, vacations and sick time are just a part of it. Many corporations say that a staff person costs them approximately 30% to 40% more than the salary. Within the design field, the cost is very similar.

Before adding a new employee, do a break-even analysis on this person and all his costs to be sure you can really afford him. Be sure that the person you are hiring fits in with your business goal.

You may discover as I did that your present staff is really not what you need. It is nice to have a certain person because he makes your studio look very nice, but is he producing or is he just there for cosmetic purposes? How much is cosmetic worth? Is it part of your image, your advertising? Each of us must evaluate this on a regular basis and be sure that our employees continue to fit the business objectives of our company.

Most interior design firms' objectives vary considerably from one decade to another and very possibly your employees require altering in order to fit these goals.

126

Create a simple personnel manual. Write down what is expected of employees. Describe their jobs. Define the employee's position within the company, his wages, his promotion opportunity, and just who he is responsible to in the company and what decisions he is responsible for. Outline his benefits, such as vacations, holidays, time off, define his working hours, when he will be paid, if he is paid any overtime.

It is helpful to have these written down and defined and to review them when you are reviewing salaries. Often, when someone wants additional salary, you can perhaps make some adjustments on these areas in order to be able to afford to handle this.

Sometimes employees are given benefits which they may consider of no value although they cost the company money. Small companies should review with the employee what they feel are real benefits and what they feel are really of no value.

THE MANAGING DIRECTOR

This title, I think, represents the duties of the manager within the interior design firm. He is responsible for managing and the financial direction of the company, a firm from probably three or four people up to maybe a 50-75 person firm.

We divide our firm into two parts: the designing area and the managerial and expediting division. The manager is responsible for coordinating schedules, all financial obligations of the company, any business management problem that arises; he has the ability to fire, to hire. He also has the ability to deal with most things that pertain to general financial subjects and management within the company. He deals with most of our consultants, such as our accountant, attorneys and other business professional consultants.

He has very little to do with the design end of it, but he assists in creating estimates and sets standards for mark-ups. He processes the orders and he does the expediting and any business or financial parts of the job which might be required.

The managing director should be a person with a business management background rather than an interior design orientation. If we want to make a firm financially successful, we need different outlooks on a job.

The managing director can have an MBA, although it is not necessary for running a small company. It is important that this person be familiar with the business terms appropriate to our current business vocabulary. Most interior designers are short on business education.

MOTIVATING EMPLOYEES

During the many workshops that I do, a constant question is "How do I motivate my employees?" Motivation can be learned. It is not something that has to be totally inborn, but it does help. It is important for the principal of the firm, or the managing personality, to be highly motivated themselves. If they are not, it is impossible to trigger it in other people.

Psychologists tell us that we must see ourselves being successful, see ourselves completing something in a superior fashion before we will ever be able to accomplish it. The imagery factor is important, especially to interior designers.

HIRING NEW EMPLOYEES

Before making the decision to hire a new employee, define carefully what the job requires. What will make this person successful in this particular project? Create a job outline so that when interviewing an employee, you are sure of exactly what you require. Then find the person who has the best qualifications to meet the success of this list of requirements.

So often we look for people that we like or people we think would fit the image of our company and do not consider carefully the objectives of that particular position.

When hiring a new employee, one very successful way of finding out whether they will work with your team is to try them on a design project. If someone is not working, he is very happy to come aboard to work on a single project. This helps you evaluate the quality of his design work, the type of personality he has, whether he will fit with your group, and many other qualifications that you would never be able to discover through a standard resume or a portfolio. Some of the best matches in the field have been acquired through a situation where one designer saw another's technician working on a project or had the opportunity of working with him and then suggesting that they work together.

Selecting employees is often said to be more dramatic than a good marriage.

INDEPENDENT CONTRACTORS

Using an independent contractor to handle parts of your requirements is advantageous to the small interior design firm. An independent contractor is not subject to conventional benefits and obligations that are present in a normal employer-employee relationship. You do not have them on your payroll every week; they pay all their individual expenses; you are contracting just for the task that is required. You have the opportunity of estimates ahead and a formal quotation rather than a project being done in-house and very often having difficulty in determining just the amount of labor required on the project.

Time Equals Money

Your income is based on time. In my experience, only 20% of the time spent on a project is responsible for 80% of the design-productive results. By the same token, 80% of the time produces 20% of the resulting design. Very few people deliberately set out to waste time, but most of us will put off doing something because we feel we don't do it as well as we would like to.

A laissez-faire attitude, taking things as they come, may make you an easy person to be around, but it doesn't automatically make you a good business person. To take advantage of opportunities as they come up, you need to be prepared for them, by having a structure in your business dealings and by being aware of potential time-wasters.

MEETINGS

We have to attend many meetings and some prove to be a waste of time. If you have an outline of what you hope to do at the meeting and a list of questions you wanted answered, you may save yourself from having to go to another meeting. The timing of the meeting can also work against you. We've all been to meetings where we weren't sure what we wanted to accomplish because we had not had time to plan for them.

CORRESPONDENCE

In our office, we phone whenever we can instead of writing letters. When you include the cost of secretarial and executive time in the cost of a letter, you see that a telephone call almost anywhere in the U.S. is no more expensive. And telephone calls are a two-way situation; they eliminate weeks of letter writing. Sometimes you can answer a letter with a line or two at the bottom of the page, and it can leave your office within minutes instead of whenever a secretary gets time to type it. Whenever you do this, keep a copy in your file.

SALES REPRESENTATIVE

We need them as much as we need the time that seeing them takes away from a project. In our office, we control the time by giving sales representatives the conference room to set up in. The samples and presentation are ready when the designers come into the room. Designers can come and go at will.

TRAVEL

Though necessary, travel eats time. When calculating the cost of an out-of-town job, remember to include travel time. I live in Harrisburg, two hours away from Philadelphia. Round trip represents half a day's work. If I can read a book or magazine or write business letters, I'm ahead.

SEARCHING FOR SOURCES

Without our reference material, we are handicapped. A file of resource material is an inexpensive but valuable tool. I realize it takes time to set one up, but if you are giving shelf space to resource items, it makes sense to have them organized. Sort through them annually to remove items or catalogues inappropriate to your design practice. As new material comes in, review it critically in terms of what you know about the manufacturer and whether you will use the product. If you won't use it regularly, either file it with other rarely used but needed material or dispose of it.

TELEPHONE

The telephone is a valuable commodity and a tremendous waste of time. Keep a three-minute egg timer by the telephone and time your conversations. It may not immediately reduce the time you spend on the phone, but you will be more aware of the passing of time. Try to establish a time of day to make your calls. The chapter on telephone use contains more ways to make phone time count.

TIME SAVERS

Planning and organizing takes time, but can help you use time more effectively. Your office is your best time-saving tool. Plan and equip it as if it were for a client.

Plan your day the night before with a list of your daily tasks, and group similar tasks.

Organize activities by the name of the person to be dealt with on each issue. When you talk with that person, you can cover all the issues that involve him.

Rank each activity or task on a scale of one to four; urgent, very important, necessary but not immediate, helpful but optional. Be sure to do several urgent items each day.

Establish deadlines for yourself, for your staff, and for the people doing your contracting services.

Keep a weekly time sheet and have each member of your staff do the same. There are several standard time sheets listing appointments, hours, expenses, clients, etc., so you can cost out your job from them. At the end of the week, summarize the projects still in the works and include notes on anything that interfered with your finishing them. Our time sheet is at the end of the chapter.

Learn to use small blocks of time rather than waiting for the precise perfect moment; it may never come. Figure out which jobs can be done in two or three minutes and do them waiting for a client or a phone call.

Clean off your desk. I think much more clearly when working on a single project. Unfortunately, our field has few standard sizes and shapes, so we need an organized way to deal with samples, catalogues and other components that cross the desk.

The noon hour can be a good time to get a few extra things done. In our studio we often meet at lunch to talk over what we have done and what snags we've run into. It helps us outline our objectives for the afternoon.

Learn to say no to projects which do not contribute to your design goals.

Do your contractors understand the drawings and instructions you give them? Try to match the complexity of the project to the skill of a particular contractor.

134

Getting started in the morning can be hard for some people. If you are one of them, leave a half-finished project on your desk to work on the next morning. It gives you a great feeling of accomplishment to have been in the office just a few minutes and to have already finished something.

At the end of the week, make a list of incomplete projects, so you know what you have to do in the next week.

Quick turnaround is an economics phrase that also applies to design work. The longer a project remains in your studio, the less profitable it is. See what you can do to improve the design studio time, to improve each step of expediting. If a phone call will make it move faster, telephone.

How precise should a time sheet be? One that works for me is a 9×12-inch diary sheet on which I list everything I do during a day. Every phone call and every person I speak to is on that sheet. The book is like my right arm; it goes with me wherever I go. I refer to it whenever there is a question such as: Did I talk to a client on Tuesday morning? The entry may say I called the client at 9:37 a.m. and got no answer so I called again at 3:30 p.m. I also note ahead for things scheduled.

Time and the way it is managed contribute to your success. It has taken years of study to become a designer, years of work and research and image building for the design field to get where it is today. We must use every moment of our working days in as professional a manner as possible. If you are not organized and cannot expedite your jobs, you are not a professional designer.

Every hour spent is an hour of profit or loss.

135

Mary K INTERIORS, INC.

STAFF MEMBER: _____ **WEEK ENDING:** _____ 19____

	CLIENT	PROJECT	CODE	HOUR
MONDAY				
TUESDAY				
WEDNESDAY				
THURSDAY				
FRIDAY				
SATURDAY				

JOB CODES				
	C - CONFERENCE	**ES-** ESTIMATING	**O** - ORDERING	**S** - SUPERVISION
	D - DRAFTING	**EX-** EXPEDITING	**R** - RESEARCH	
	DE- DESIGNING	**I** - INSTALLATION	**SP-** SPECIFYING	

Use of the Telephone

A telephone is often easier and less expensive than writing a letter. A simple letter, at the cost of secretarial time today, is approximately $6.00 to $8.00. You can call across the country for that amount of money and have an immediate reply. We use the telephone constantly in our office. We want to know if merchandise is available or not and the telephone is one of the least expensive means of communication we have.

Within your personal telephone directory, it is important to name the person who is most effective at each of your sources. Knowing the right person to talk to can save many hours and much confusion. Also, many of our companies today have Wats lines and the 800 numbers do save us a considerable amount of money. So, use these when they are available. If you do not find a Wats line available, many times it is better to go ahead and make the call rather than waste another 15 or 20 minutes. At designers' rates, this can be quite expensive.

We found a personal Wats line for our company to be too costly since we really do not call one area but many parts of the United States and therefore require an extensive service. At the moment, we do not have that service, but we are looking forward to having one sometime in the future.

Train your personnel to use the telephone properly. Proper terminology on the telephone helps to motivate people to give a positive attitude for your company. Terms like "will you, help me, I'm sorry, please, if you would be so very kind, it's been a great pleasure"; a few seconds of courtesies, either to clients or to our sources, can build a warm relationship and can inspire them to be of assistance in the future.

I attempt to make many of my telephone calls to contractors before 9:00 a.m. I find that they are often available that time and it saves a great deal of time later in the day. If you have a standard time available when people know they can reach you, such as in my case—the contractors can reach me between 7:00 and 8:30 a.m. most mornings—all of these calls are completed before you begin your day's work. It saves a great deal of interruption during the day.

CONFERENCE CALLS

Conference calls are very important and an inexpensive way of managing many details that can only be accomplished by getting two or three people together. There are a number of systems available—either through your telephone company or individual companies—which enable you to have a conference call with two, three or more people throughout the country. How inexpensive this is compared to bringing three or four people to one central location.

Who should answer your telephone? It is better if you have a long-time employee, someone who is familiar with your organization, to answer the phone. This will save you so much time in passing telephone calls from person to person. So many companies use their newest and lowest paid employee, and this is a really bad mistake. Try to eliminate waste in time of both your client and your staff by having a knowledgeable person answering your telephone.

Answering services are also a very valuable thing for many designers. Select your answering service with great care because they are representing you. Improper conduct by an answering service can really do a great deal to destroy professionalism.

I think answering services are preferable to answering machines. However, I must say that answering machines are often the difference between reaching someone or not reaching them. There is nothing worse than needing to talk with someone and having no possible way of getting to them. When you leave messages on an answering machine, state the time you will be available so that you do not call back and forth with no reply.

Handle your telephone as professionally as you handle every other part of your business. Time spent on the phone is just as expensive as time spent interacting with a client or on the drafting table. Learn to limit your calls, perhaps by having an egg timer on your desk.

When I begin a phone call, I mark down on my diary what time I begin and what time I finish. If I find a call is taking more time than it should, I will often say something like, "Excuse me, please, but I have a call on the other line." Or, "I have a problem I have to take care of immediately, may I call you back?" or "Is there anything else we must cover now? Can we take this up later?" There are polite ways of ending a call.

I will take a call from any contractor who is working on a project at almost any time of the day, even when I am with clients. The client I am working with now would not want to think his job would cost more money because I would not be available to the contractor when he needed me. We try to have several people here in the office who can handle questions regarding jobs but they will interrupt me if they cannot handle it. Calls from another client or a salesperson, etc., are held and the people are informed that "Mary will return your call today at 4:30 p.m. or she will return your call tomorrow."

When you call and find no one there and you are going to leave a message, be sure to leave your name and telephone number, but also the reason for your call so that the person who is receiving the phone call can have time to prepare the answer. When they call you back, they will have the information and it will not cost you an additional delay or waste of time.

If you receive phone calls at an inconvenient time, it is a good idea to ask the caller how long he estimates the call will take. If you do not have the time then, ask him if he will call you another time, or *you* will return the call when it is convenient.

Inform the caller that you are in the middle of a very difficult task before he gets to his subject and suggest the call should be rescheduled.

SHOULD A BUSINESS
PURCHASE ITS OWN TELEPHONE?

When we moved into our building, we priced it both ways—the Bell Telephone Company and also an outside firm. If you think you are going to require this type of service for a 7-10 year period, it pays you to consider purchasing your own equipment. We were not sure that our needs would be exactly the same a few years from now since it was a different facility and a different form of doing business. We did not purchase our own equipment, but this very definitely can prove a savings. You can also have many other advantages and extras on your line if you have purchased it rather than using a standard system.

MOBILE TELEPHONE

I have a mobile phone in my car and find it most convenient. I can call anywhere in the United States or anywhere that you dial on your regular telephone. I find this time saving. Mobile phones are not available in all areas and are somewhat impractical in larger cities since there are so many people using the channels. Check your area. It may prove to be economical and a convenient tool if you are driving as many miles per year as I am, approximately 35,000 to 40,000 miles a year. So, I do spend a lot of time in my car. Not only does it save me time, it makes me feel just a bit safer when I am out on the highway alone.

I purchased my mobile phone and I am sure it is now more than paid for. You can rent one through your telephone company or purchase one outright from Motorola Corporation.

Reference Organization

One of the key information sources for interior designers is their filing system. It is important to have timely and accurate information available to us at all times. In order to do this, we must have an efficient management system of our resources. There is no question that the demands for information in a design firm today are greater than at any other time in history.

Interior designers have catalogs, clippings, photographs, tearsheets; they have a regular record system including active records and inactive records. Some may even include computer technology, microfilm, and microfiche, although this is a relatively new thing for the interior designer. Of course, we all have libraries which we have treasured through the years.

SOURCE FILES

Catalogs are one of our main sources of information about the products we require for our clients. Manufacturers and distributors are usually pleased to put them into our hands. We review each catalog and its source before we put it on our shelf. There is no point in storing something that really is inappropriate for your interior design practice. We review the company as to their quality of product, their expediting procedures as well as cost factors, design and other necessary reviews.

One of the key points in a filing system is good indexing. It must be arranged so that material can be obtained very quickly. The following is an example of how you might index your different products. For example, under *flooring materials*, carpeting, ceramic, vinyl, wood, and others are to be listed.

Under office furnishings, you would sub-classify into desks, executive, secretarial, general staff areas or work areas, and then break it down further into types of materials and styles within each one of these categories.

Each file will vary considerably as to the sources you will eventually use. Be sure that the people who are using the files establish the indexing so that they will know exactly where to go for each particular area.

Arrange all your *product catalogs* by the vendor's name. Keep the company's catalogs together. Very often, additional information regarding products is required and it is helpful to have the complete issue together. Be sure that your cross index file identifies the products and classifies them in every category that would be appropriate.

Open shelves are most successful for *catalog files*. They probably hold more per square foot than other storage, but you do need standard filing drawers for file folders and details that cannot be accommodated on shelves.

Photographs, clippings and tearsheets are often part of a presentation to a client. Index them in a similar fashion to the way that you have indexed your major catalogs. Keep them completely separate, perhaps by using a different color file so that they are in no way confused with current material.

Store photographs between some form of stiffener and be sure that they are kept in a file which is compressed in order to prevent curling of the photographs.

Never write on photographs; indentify them with another form of labeling. If photographs are properly cared for, they can have an extended life and a long usage. Similar indexing can be used for these as for the catalog files.

OPERATING RECORDS

Your operating records are the memory bank of your practice. They are essential to an efficient and profitable management of your design company.

Your *active records* would include your clients' design record (usually indexed by projects or in alphabetical order by the client's name). It is often helpful to keep the current project separate from the completed projects.

Your *accounting records* should be indexed by categories: accounts receivable, accounts payable, your payroll. These should be maintained by calendar or by fiscal year.

Your operational records should be indexed by classification: administration, legal, marketing, planning, financial, sales. I suggest that you do not have too many categories but do subdivide them so that you can handle one issue at a time.

Your art work and drawings are best kept in flat files designed for them. If these are not available, drawings should be rolled and clearly labelled on the tubes in which they are stored.

In order to meet government regulations and also support other management decisions in the future, you must keep certain records for a scheduled length of time. Have your accountant review this with you according to your individual state and federal requirements.

Many storage cabinets are available for inactive files and these can often be kept up off the premises in order to permit for current files to be most accessible.

Identify and be sure that *inactive files* are accessible. Keep a log so that you know exactly where these are, and each file should state the name and the type of records which it holds.

You should have a complete file of all inactive files, exactly where they are stored, and what is in each one so that whenever references are required, it is not a question of searching. This can be done by merely keeping one simple file.

Many medium to larger businesses are working with computers now, often on a timesharing basis, for inventory, accounts receivable, accounts payable. There are now many, many computers that are inexpensive and can be purchased by an interior designer. This is an ever-changing area and should be reviewed for the possible adaptation to the interior design business.

Microfilm and microfiche are another new medium. ASID is presently working on a microfiche program which could be one of the most exciting programs that have touched our field in many years. It is such a convenient system to bring many new products to each of us for very simple and easy reference.

An interior design library should have: catalog files, reference books and text, directories, professional journals, periodicals, reference reports; your material sources such as carpets, fabrics, finishes and other materials that are part of the design project. There are many ways of filing this type of material and they do become very cumbersome and difficult in some instances. We prefer our fabrics folded rather than on hangers. We store everything according to category. Every sample is coded so that it automatically returns to the exact bin. All of the fabrics are placed according to style and character of material so that when you are researching contemporary upholstery fabrics, you know exactly which piles are appropriate for this kind of material.

We find it very cumbersome and almost unprofessional to use hangers. We find the folded storage method which is somewhat old-fashioned is still one of the most convenient methods for our design studio. It also permits us to bring to the client what we want to show them and not expose the client at any point to a large collection of materials.

Our library is kept off bounds to clients because it is something that the designers use for reference.

We also use a very simple storage cabinet for our 3"×5" carpet samples. Each type of carpet and color is classified according to style and color, so that if you want a blue residential carpet, you merely pull out a drawer and you have all the blue carpet. If you are dealing with contract carpet and you want a certain specification for a hospital use, there are drawers for those; you go to the drawer and pull the samples out immediately.

We also have many wallcovering books which are stored on open shelves, again according to companies. We find this the easiest way to identify these.

Paint samples, laminate samples and other general materials are stored either in drawers or in open shelving.

We find that our library is best close to our designer's work area so it is convenient for them to pull materials as required.

Within the areas of samples and catalogs, it is important to have established review time. We check our samples twice a year; our catalogs are reviewed on an annual basis, and this is absolutely necessary in maintaining a reasonably up-to-date sample file. We have one person who has the responsibility of this, and it is her job to review all of these things on a regular basis. It keeps her busy approximately two to three days per week on an annual basis.

Inventory

Some designers have a great deal of inventory and work for furniture companies where they are actually buying and selling furniture. Others acquire some inventory in accessories, paintings and other art objects they feel will work into future projects. Is it really to our advantage financially to have this inventory or is it undermining our profit structure?

Inventory today is *expensive*. I don't think this can be overemphasized. Inventory costs a minimum of 15%, at the average annual interest rate. The insurance probably runs another 2 to 3% of the inventory per year. In addition, there is the cost of dusting, handling storage and a certain amount of breakage. Every object you inventory costs you between *25-30% to hold on to for one year.* If you have the object three years, you must be able to add 30% per year to continue to own that object at a profitable rate. Although we experience inflation, I doubt that we can afford to increase our prices to compensate.

I am amazed at how many designers of sizeable consequence are not aware of these figures. The founder of one of the larger design firms not too long ago told me that she buys antiques in Europe and sells them through her studio. She restores the pieces before selling them, but she has to keep many for several years before finding the appropriate client. She felt she had an excellent profit on these items. At that time I was using the figures of 26-28% cost per year for inventory. She realized that what *she* thought was profit may or may not have been profit. She was paying for it in another form.

So, I suggest you look at your inventory, assess its true value and its potential. Be sure that it really contributes to the profit of your design business. You may be better off with this money in your active account, or investing it where you can earn 15% a year. As designers, we must carefully review all parts of our business to be sure each one of them adds up to a better quality design as well as a total profit.

Client Communication

The initial interview is your client's first opportunity to see you as a person and the interior design field as a profession. It is also your first chance to assess the client. Although the term personality clash is a bit of a cliché, you should take it into consideration. After all, you are going to be working closely with these people for an extended period of time, and you need a good rapport.

Research is something I recommend to every designer. Before going to a prospective client, I try to find out as much about him as possible. For a contract or commercial project, I always run a credit review on the firm. I also want to have some idea of its objectives and to know the involvement of other professionals in the project. I do this through reading Dun & Bradstreet reports, and by talking with other contractors. I look over the building reports, which tell you that contracts have been let on a particular building for construction work, electrical wiring, and plumbing, to the tune of $24 million. This gives me some idea of what kind of budget I will be working with. I find out who the principals in the firm are. When I walk in for the first interview, I understand who is in charge, their accomplishments and interests.

After you have researched the project, make yourself an outline. A businessman outlines his objectives for every meeting; so should the professional designer. In the initial interview you need to determine the scope of the project: the client's needs, scheduling, financial expectations and restraints.

One of the first things I ask a prospective client is what he knows about our firm and where he heard of us. It is important for the client to know something about the designer, to understand if possible the techniques and procedures in which you work. It helps when a client has been in a home or an office you designed, and it helps when he has talked to a former client. Sometimes a former client can better explain your working procedure than you, especially if he is an attorney talking to another attorney, or a banker talking to another banker. Interior design is a strange service to many people, and I find it complicates the job when the client has no idea of what design services are.

The location of the initial interview is a matter of personal preference. I hold my initial interviews on the job site so I can see some of the particulars and review the client's experience. Has he worked with another designer and did he like their work? Seeing where and how the client lives or works helps me determine what design standard to work from. I want all the visual clues possible. If a person says he wants to redo his office inexpensively, I have no idea what he means until I have seen the space. If the room is done in one-of-a-kind pieces, and the client wants to scale down, I still have a workable budget.

To charge or not to charge for the first interview is the perennial question. I have heard designers say they wouldn't walk out of the studio without being paid for their time, but my policy is usually not to charge for the first interview. It is my opportunity to look over the space and the situation and to determine whether I want the job. I've walked into situations that I felt were inappropriate to my practice. Because I did not charge, I have felt free to walk out.

One of my colleagues, who earned an impressive sum of money on what sounded like a highly creative project, told me that the aggravations, anxiety and utter frustration she endured totalled ten times what she had been paid. Although the idea of turning down a wealthy would-be client on a lucrative venture might seem foolish, think again. No amount of money can compensate for the emotional strain and physical upsets some people seem to generate.

I recall visiting a potential client in a magnificant and well-appointed residence and being offered a remodelling job that I really thought would fit my design style. We were interrupted by two phone calls which she took in the kitchen. I heard, "Sue him!" and "Don't take anything from him!" After the second "Take him to court!" I figured I had better tread carefully because I was obviously dealing with an exceptionally litigious person. Who could say I wouldn't be the third, fourth or fifth person she decided to sue this month? I managed to bow out of the job and later learned that the designer who had accepted it wound up in the middle of a lawsuit.

Other people seem to attract suits against them. One doctor client of mine amassed an unpaid account of over

$30,000 before I took it to my attorney. He discovered that there were 16 suits of this sort against this doctor—a man who loudly proclaimed he earned more money than any other doctor in town! This man, whose income was in the hundreds of thousands of dollars, didn't really understand that the ten or fifteen thousand dollars he owed contractors may have represented their profit for the year. He also had no respect for anyone who was not in the medical profession.

Trust your gut reactions. It's not always easy to spot the potential problem client, but the first rule of interviewing is to trust your gut reactions. Our initial responses to people are based on nonverbal clues, things we sense without being aware of the source or reasons.

Probe the humor index. The things that amuse us or fail to amuse us tap our deepest prejudices and values. Arm yourself with a few quips and funny stories. If your prospective client reacts blandly, the prognosis is not good. If he or she responds negatively, it is definitely not good.

Assess the empathy level. Every designer has a story or two about things that went wrong on the job, whether it was an Act of God, a personal miscalculation, or a factory error. Someone who says, "That better not happen on my job!" or is overly critical of the event is probably a client you would want to send to a competitor of whom you are not too fond. Here, you need to look for some expression of sympathy or understanding, a viewpoint that reflects tolerance.

Use the "what if" probe. This strategy is intended to determine the client's reactions to frustrations and disappointments. You might believe you can meet your client's expressed deadline of Christmas time, but you also know that things can go wrong. Using the what if probe, you might say, "I'm pretty sure everything will be finished by

154

Christmas, but I don't have control of every link in the chain. All sorts of things can go wrong—strikes, floods, factory errors—and could delay completion. Being optimistic, I don't think they will, but what if they do?"

Listen to their words. The words you need to be most aware of are: should, ought, must, have to, and their opposites. The *must* and *should* types betray a lack of flexibility and penchant for rage and unreasonable demands. Quite often inflexible people have learned to mask their aggressive feelings with a facade of cordiality and superficial responsibility. But they cannot hide the manner in which their underlying hostilities slip out in their conversation: "You must be sure that the project is complete by the 14th." It may be said pleasantly, with a warm, friendly smile, but it contains the give-away "must." Take notice.

There are many, many individual interview techniques. No matter which you use, it helps to keep a list of the ones that work for you on your interviewing sheet with the outline of the questions you want answered. In effect, use the initial interview not just to learn what the client needs and wants and can afford, but also to learn about the client. The best way to do it is to ask questions and to listen carefully. Observe. Question. Probe. Don't always offer an opinion or make a judgment. Try to be neutral. Smile or nod, and watch the body language of your client.

Use short verbal probes: yes, sure, right, of course. Try state probes: How do you feel? What do you think about this?

Use echo probes: Repeat what the client says, to encourage him to develop on the theme. Or return to an issue you have already discussed, a reflective probe.

I have talked about studying the client's language for personality clues. Does your own language say what you mean, or is it open to interpretation? A single comment can influence or color the whole job. You should aim for simplicity and clarity in everything you do and say, because most clients do not understand the design field or its vocabulary. When discussing sizes, always relate them to something the client has in his home or office, something he is familiar with and can visualize. Early in my career I learned never to embarrass a client by using the jargon of interior design. It doesn't make you superior. It just makes the client feel inferior, and this does not help a sale or foster rapport.

The way you look and dress is critical; you never know what you may have to buy with your appearance. If you appear to come from a different world from your clients, they may find it difficult to relate to you. You are there to create a liaison, and the way you look is part of the presentation. I am more comfortable in simple fashions, although some designers prefer flamboyance. This must fit your personality and the type of presentation proposed.

Your presentation must include carefully researched written cost estimates and a time schedule. If cost revisions are later required because of a substantial design change, put the changes and the cost revision in writing. Explain your expectations—income or retainer—but present this in writing also. Don't complain that someone is not paying you when you have not carefully outlined your financial expectations.

Outline your interview — before going to any interview or meeting, establish and list your goals.

Leave nothing to chance. So often, we get into a meeting, get sidetracked on a particular issue, and go home without covering the important issues at hand. Unless I have made a checklist ahead of just what I expect to accomplish and maintain some control of the time structure during the meeting, they (the meetings) tend not to accomplish what I had intended. Keep your checklist with you during the course of the meeting and mark next to each statement your answers for later references. Not only does this save time, but it also helps considerably with one's professional appearance.

The Twilight Zone

The twilight zone begins when the client approves the initial project and ends when it is delivered. This is the time that causes so much anxiety to both the designer and the client. By structuring the communications during this period, you can improve your client's feelings toward you as a professional, as well as keep them reasonably contented and pleased during the expediting period.

It is often said that the design job is 10% design and 90% the ability to expedite and to execute the final project. The twilight zone is where many designers fall down. We were all well trained in the 10% area, but lacked orientation for expediting.

With each new client, we establish a definite communication schedule for the duration of the job. Once a week on a given day—we check with the client to find out which day and what time is convenient—they will receive a call from our office, either from the designer who is working on the job or from the Managing Director who is responsible for expediting the project. On that day, they will get an up-dated report of exactly where the job is and in what stage of completion. Early in the job there is often not much to report. You may simply call the client and say, "All the purchase orders have been placed for your job."

One of our policies, in addition to a written order, is to phone in the order to see if any items have been discontinued or if there is anything incorrect or incomplete about our purchase order. We might explain to our client that the orders have been placed and we have no problem on the job or that we do see one fabric that is discontinued and, therefore, we require another selection. When can we arrange an appointment to make that selection?

Each job has a master sheet. On it we outline the job to be done and where each part of the job is standing at that particular time. The telephone call is made with our master sheet in front of us. Simple record keeping is on the back of the master sheet; our Managing Director notes any comments that the client may have regarding the telephone conversations with them. This means that in addition to the master file with all the original specifications, we have a complete rundown on exactly what is being done and all conversations and all data. So, if the designer wants to know what the Managing Director has said to a client, he merely picks up the master sheet. He can see exactly where the order stands, the acknowledgements, whether the merchandise has been received, and what interaction the Managing Director has had with the client.

When we make a presentation, we give the client an outline of the time schedule. It states when the materials are expected, as well as when the different crafts people will be working in their space. If revisions are required or a final date is set, we tell the client during our weekly report. We will additionally send them an updated outline of time expectancies so that they are aware of the preparation that is required in order to have the space ready for our crafts people when they arrive on the job.

The client is aware that once a week on a given day, they will hear from us. This eliminates our getting many calls throughout the week. It also permits us to pull the client file to have up-to-date information on that client, and be able to speak intelligently about his job. So often when one is interrupted in the middle of another client's interview or while doing another project, your mind is not on the caller's project and you may have to guess. When you have the opportunity of pulling it all together, you can give them much more accurate information.

We talk weekly to the other professionals involved on the job, such as architect, engineers, or job coordinators. Neglecting this communication destroys cooperation and can undermine the project.

This regular interaction not only serves to support professionalism but is an excellent market tool. If clients are aware that you are on top of their job and they are receiving very special, personal care, this is impressive. They are very quick to recommend someone who they feel has given them very strong and definite attention.

We find that this can sometimes spur clients on to do parts of the project that they had not considered earlier. They realize that the project is moving along smoothly. It is not interfering extremely with their way of life. They are prepared and expect what is going to happen and, therefore, they will very often consider going further with a project.

EXPEDITING

What happens to an order from the time the order is placed until the product is delivered? During this period of order development, small things can either make or destroy an order, a product, as well as a client relationship. Communication should be regular during this period. This is just as important as the initial acquiring of an order and development of the design.

Part of the ability to get the job completed, of course, falls within designing something that is practical within the medium in which you are working. I mean the craftsmen that you have available as well as your staff.

You must carefully consider the materials that you use when you look at the time limit. Can you afford to specify materials from all parts of the world when you only have 90 days to expedite a job? Initially, when the expediting gets an order, the design has been completed and there is an expected delivery date on the project. This date is established between the designer and the client. The expediter knows that the client is expecting this order in three months, in six months, in a year. It could be any length of time, running from two weeks to a year or longer. Few orders are done in a period of two weeks.

Everything you consider on this project is based on date of completion. As an example, an order comes in having 20-30 parts. An order may have fabric, labor and other materials going into that chair or item. The expediter would place the order for each and every material required.

The order would be marked with the date the order is required, one copy of the purchase order is attached to the initial workorder. One copy of the purchase order is placed in your "On Order" file. This means that you have a

162

file made up in alphabetical order of each and every company that you have things ordered from. When you get an invoice in from Fabric Company A, you go to that order file and match the invoice with the order.

On your purchase order, you have the name of the client and the purchase order number. The work order number that we start out with on our work order follows through on all the purchase orders. This means if a work order is 9046, all the purchaser order numbers would be 9046A, B, C, D, etc.

The order is placed. In approximately a week to ten days, you should have an acknowledgement or some confirmation. This will tell you if the fabric is available; you may have an invoice for it at that point. If it is not available, it will be four to six weeks. It will be three months.

You immediately compare all acknowledgements with your delivery expectations. If you have a year to deliver a product and there is a three-month delay in the fabric, since you know it only takes another 30-60 days to produce the sofa after you have the fabric, it really doesn't matter. But, if you have an acknowledgement which says that the delivery of this fabric will be 60 days and the client is expecting it in 90 days, you had better do some checking. Even though you have a 30-day cushion, you really can't count on that. They mean they are expecting that fabric from the mill on that date. They are not expecting it to be delivered in your hands then. The fabric might be coming from England or Ireland: it may be a situation of shipping delay to them as well as shipping delay from the company to us.

At this point, it is important to bring the delay to the attention of the designer in charge. Most likely, the designer will say, "Well, I know that I have a fabric almost identical to that from another firm. Let's consider using the Fabric Company B fabric instead of the Fabric Company A fabric." So, she will in turn pull out the two fabrics, decide whether this is a reasonable choice, check it through with the client. If the client approves the change, then change the fabric from Fabric Company A to Fabric Company B.

Now, when we change the fabric, what has to happen? The order in this case was for a sofa which went to an upholsterer. The upholsterer is expecting a fabric from Fabric Company A with a certain number. You must write them and tell them they are not going to be receiving that fabric. Because it is discontinued, they will be receiving a Fabric Company B fabric. *Before* you do ANY changes, you confirm that you have the Fabric Company B fabric. It is pointless to write all those orders and do all that paper work if you are not sure you have that second fabric.

Suppose a client decides there is no substitute for her fabric and the designer feels it is really important. The designer will call Mrs. Long and say, "Mrs. Long, the particular fabric you ordered, which is imported from England, is delayed by approximately two months. Are you willing to wait?" And Mrs. Long is going to say yes or no. Then an adjustment is going to have to be made on the overall order if she changes the fabric and you, therefore, have to change something else. It may not be a matter of just changing sofa fabrics; it may mean changing the draperies, accent pillows, or three or four other things that go with the fabric that you are changing.

Or Mrs. Long knows that she is waiting and is prepared to wait. That's fine. Because she has been informed, and she has been informed at the early part of the job and the client has made that decision. When the client has the choice, it makes it much better.

The other follow-up procedures that I think are important are, each and every week, on an appropriate day—and I would suggest it be the same day every week—you go over every client order and every piece of merchandise that is on order, and see if there is anything that you do not have acknowledgement on. See if there was anything that was expected in 60 days, but now it is 75 days. See if there is anything that is not measuring out to our expected delivery requirements. If there is something that is not measuring out, it is my suggestion that these people either be contacted by telephone (I'm speaking about companies) or by letter so that you know why that is delayed, what the problem is and you are on top of it, just in case that order was never received. Just in case there is a mistake on it. Just in case the order is lost. It is caught now, not three weeks into the order, not 90 days into the order when it should be on your loading dock. Cover your companies in that fashion. Really go over those orders periodically, at least once a week, because if you go over them every week, you know what happened last week. There is no point in checking on this because he says there is nothing going to happen in 60 days, or nothing is going to happen for 30 days. You will spot very quickly your five, six, or eight problems and you will know what ones you should watch.

Another thing that I think is important is that each and every client be called once a week and given a report on their order. My reason for this is, it makes the company look like we are really on our toes, like we have been checking records.

Master Sheet

Mary K INTERIORS, INC.
2901 N. Front Street Harrisburg, Penna.

CLIENT: _____

ADDRESS: _____

PHONE NUMBER: _____

DATE: _____

DESIGNER: _____

Date	Order Number	Supplier	Item	Expected Shipping	Received	Delivered	Billed	Remarks

Installation, Complaint Handling and Follow-Up

THE INSTALLATION

The installation is one of the strongest selling parts of a job. We are constantly selling a project through the way we handle the job—not just in the initial interview or in the presentation, but the whole way through the "twilight zone" and on into the installation. The way we handle a job and the manner in which our craft people work in a person's facility determine the quality of design work.

The question, to install all at one time or to do a project piecemeal, is sometimes not the designer's decision. If we can arrange to install a project all at one time, or to coordinate tightly the crafts people with the installation of furniture, do it. This definitely makes a difference in the impact of the design on the client. Seeing something

167

piecemeal does not give the client the full idea of what we are attempting to accomplish. If we can arrange to do the job at one time, it always helps our professional image.

Many designers require that the clients not be on site during the installation days; they take the property over completely. I think this is desirable if it can be arranged. We attempt to have a person on site throughout the installation, if at all possible, or at least we have someone constantly checking on the installation to be sure that the crafts people are maintaining the standards that we want them to.

WHITE GLOVE DELIVERY

White glove delivery, defined by gentlemen who do deliveries wearing white gloves and very often white uniforms, is very impressive and I think is coming back. Why? Because so many of the items we are installing are very precious and very expensive. We can't emphasize enough that everyone who is working on a client's job is concerned with product and the finished design. It is a critical point in client interaction. They consider their office space or their homes precious parts of their lives. When we display our concern, it leads to a better interaction between clients and designer. If you can design a "white glove delivery" for your clients, I think you will find that it pays off in avoiding complaints and in making a client pleased with his project.

HANDLING COMPLAINTS

The way one handles a complaint could be the single strongest point in demonstrating professionalism to clients. More projects are made by handling a complaint properly than probably any other single thing we can measure. Again, the ability of a designer to show concern for the client, the ability of the designer to represent the client in handling a complaint properly, is extremely important.

Solve the problem before the client is aware of it. See that merchandise is inspected properly before delivery so that we can avoid clients being aware of any problem that is not necessary. We all know that we must cover our delivery by having a very good repair service available to us. See that everything is done and things are touched up and taken care of before the client sees it. It shows we care.

Installing everything at one time will avoid a tremendous amount of complaints.

I think that a designer's attitude toward handling complaints and working with the client is extremely important. If you have built up rapport by handling the "twilight zone" properly and the client is aware that you are on top of their project, handling the complaints will also prove easier. Just remember, every time you let a complaint hang, your client could be telling at least 20-30 potential clients. This can prove disastrous to any practice. So, the minute you hear of a complaint, take care of it. If it can be taken care of within the hour, please do it. If not, within twenty-four hours. Make it standard practice within your company that every complaint is handled within a twenty-four hour period, or at least reviewed within this period.

EVALUATION

After a project is completed, you summarize it on an evaluation sheet. Outline just how you feel this project was handled. Discuss it with your client and see if their expectations have been met. Can you expect the referrals from the client?

This summary evaluation sheet will help you in determining your future market. If the project moved smoothly, your hours spent on the project and the profit rewards as well as your design expectations have been met, and the client's needs have also been met—probably your firm is capable of handling this type of job and should continue to market for this type of project. Evaluating a project must be done close to the time of the completion of the job.

FOLLOW-UP

Your first follow-up should be approximately thirty days after the job has been completed. Do another in sixty days to ninety days. This excellent marketing tool lets the client know that you are interested in his project after it is over. It also helps you to evaluate whether the job has really met the needs of the client. After a project has been used for a period of time, you can see whether you have been able to improve their lifestyle or their working style, or whether they have reverted back to some of their older habits. Maybe you have missed certain points in the design. This evaluation is a very good learning tool for the designer as well as a strong marketing tool.

Freight Claims

At one point, freight claims were a major aggravation for our firm. We reported nearly all the damage but got no compensation at all for 40% of them. Another 30% kept us busy with phone calls, letters and forms for nearly a year. We were spending about two days a week of valuable time just on freight claims. If you are going to spend $150 a week chasing freight claims, perhaps you are better off putting that $150 into repairs and calling it overhead.

Inspect all packages immediately upon their arrival. Making notes on the condition of the merchandise on the freight bill will considerably improve the possibility of collecting on a claim. It is difficult and expensive to collect on a damage claim where only cursory inspection was made and the receipt signed with the words "subject to further inspection." Such notations no longer carry any legal weight in claims.

If the carton shows the least sign of damage, have it opened in front of the driver and evaluate the damage. If it can be repaired locally, our firm accepts it and absorbs the expense. If it cannot, we refuse it and it is returned to the shipper (distributor or manufacturer). Since adopting this policy, we have had few freight claims, and all were resolved within 120 days.

When you make a claim, you must note the conditions of the shipment in detail. To properly document a freight claim you need:

1. The original bill of lading.
2. The original paid freight bill.
3. The invoice of the item.
4. The carrier's inspection report.
5. Documents supporting the repair cost and the extra freight charges.
6. The delivery receipt showing any exceptions noted at the time of delivery.
7. Pictures of the damaged goods and packaging. It is amazing the way even a simple Polaroid photograph of a damaged piece can help to expedite a freight claim.

As designers we expect the manufacturer's reputation for quality products to be based not just on the quality of the product but on the condition of that product when it is delivered to our client. Often, merchandise that left the factory in good condition is not packed adequately to ensure that it arrives at its destination in that same good condition. It is wise to inform the manufacturer about problems so that they have the necessary information to evaluate whether they should revise their design or their packaging to reduce the stress the product is subjected to, or whether they should ever use that freight company again. The more they know about our goals and problems, the better able they are to design to avoid casualties.

Try to get the manufacturer to work with you in repairing and adjusting freight claims; they really work out more satisfactorily this way. Sometimes the manufacturer will tell you to return the merchandise, that the problem will be easier and less costly to repair if their own craftsmen do it, rather than a local man who first has to determine their techniques, or their lacquer formula.

Most manufacturers will not accept merchandise for return after you have accepted it; perhaps because they consider it unsaleable. You must get permission in writing authorizing the return of the merchandise, or the manufacturer will not allow credit.

Freight companies cannot normally be held responsible for delays in delivery. Getting to know the carriers and developing a rapport with them lets you know what to expect so there is less chance of getting into difficulties. If you feel that the transportation or delivery service was not of a reasonable quality or was not done within a reasonable amount of time, make your complaint immediately, both to the carrier and to the shipper.

The designer can be held responsible for some freight problems. If the merchandise is to be delivered where there is no loading dock or where more than one person is needed to properly unload the merchandise, the designer should state this in the shipping instructions. Otherwise, they may end up with the furniture left out on the sidewalk.

Tracing shipments is a procedure instituted only after a reasonable length of time has elapsed after the known shipment date, and delivery still has not been accomplished.

Expediting is the procedure used when you want to protect the movement of a shipment while it is in transit. A request for expediting should be made before the shipment leaves the factory in case you should want to pick it up at some point or try to keep it out of a very busy port. You may know your area and therefore may better know how to route something to your destination more quickly with fewer problems.

If you need freight information, when you call the freight company, give them your name, the name of your company, the phone numbers, the shipper's name, port of origin, the description and number of pieces and the weight, the anticipated shipping date. Also, give the name of the original carrier and the number on the bill of lading. Without this information, they cannot properly check through on any calls. So, before making the phone call, be sure that you have this information together.

Concealed Damage is damage which is not immediately noticed. It is important to report this as soon after the delivery as possible. The longer the materials are in your possession, the more difficult it will be to prove the carrier is responsible.

Inspect all merchandise before placing it in stock. Notify the carrier by telephone and letter of damage. The telephone call will expedite the claim quickly, but the letter will support that you notified the carrier. Along with the letter, take a Polaroid photograph of the damage (if it will show up in this manner) and send it along to support any package involvement in this condition.

The Contractor

Interior designers specify craft performances, engineering, and other installation procedures as well as products. Know every craft person you send into a project, because these people represent you. In each design project, you are responsible for upsetting your client's environment in his home or business.

To minimize the disruption, prepare a time and expectation schedule for your clients, letting them know their obligations before and after each craft person is to work in their space. If it is a situation where an area must be cleared to accommodate a particular project, be sure the client knows about it far enough ahead of time to do it without problems. I often will suggest that a client move out of the space until the design project is finished. Why? Because it gives us, the designer and crafts people, free access to the space and the client has at the same time a

175

clean place to use while all this is going on. It is difficult to work around people and their lifestyles and still make a profit.

One of our most exciting projects was done on a nine-day construction installation schedule. It was a professional building for a firm of five optometrists and opthamologists and a staff of 30. We couldn't work around them, because one speck of dust could ruin many of their expensive instruments, some of which cost over $100,000 each. Although their per day income was $5,000, we worked out an agreement whereby they would close for nine days, beginning on Friday. We gutted the building, reconstructed the building from steel construction, plumbing, heating, electrical work, plastering and new layout of partitioning, and even wall finishes, carpet, down to the installation of the tiniest one by one-and-a-half inch drawers to hold contact lenses.

We did it in nine days by working 20 hours a day, and everyone left the project thinking it was the greatest job he had ever done. It was a very exciting project but could only have been done with crafts people used to working together. Administering and supervising this project was complex. Someone from our staff was there all the time to make on-the-spot decisions because there wasn't a spare hour. We had only one change order on the whole job and it cost less than $20.00.

The size and quality of the contracting firms you use should be carefully defined before beginning a project. Be familiar with their vocabulary so you do not ask for things foreign to their skills. Some of our crafts people are excellent at the expense of versatility. Don't ask someone who has only worked on simple or casual projects to do something that requires exceptional expertise. You had better look for a craftsman who really wants to develop precision work and fine detailing.

Our team, meaning our design firm and the crafts people and contractors who work with us, has an understanding. If anyone sees a problem in my design, he will point it out to me immediately. If I see anything wrong with their part of the project, I make it known to them. We don't want anyone to hang himself with an error because this can happen so easily to any one of us. This agreement has made us a strong team; we all like very much working together. It tends to polish up each person's craft, to the benefit of the whole group.

On exceptionally large projects, this personal interplay may not seem practical; it works for me. My projects have varied from a few thousand dollars to twenty-five million dollars and with each of my crafts people, rapport is invaluable. I advise you to talk to your contractor as much as possible. The more you know of his strengths and weaknesses, the better you can coordinate future projects.

We are a realiable source of professional criticism for crafts people, because, as designers, we see many jobs installed and we know how we want them to look. We know which items are superior and what needs polishing.

I have seen many products marketed by major sources where the end use was never considered. Fabrics have been designed and put into production which really do not look well on anything. As designers, we have the opportunity to see that products are used in the proper situation. Our interaction and involvement in the sources and the product uses are crucial.

The more designers and manufacturers and crafts people realize that we are working together for a better end product, the easier and more profitable all of our jobs will be.

Sources and
Source Communication

Our sources are our pallette. Interior designers can coordinate many different products and sources, but one weak spot can ruin a project. It is very important to establish ground rules on how to work with our sources.

Know your sources and know them well. Before you consider specifying any material for a project, investigate the company from which you intend to purchase. If it is a new account, talk to other designers. Find out what they know about the company. I don't let any of our people use a firm which has not been thoroughly investigated.

When a new catalog comes across your desk, examine it. Be sure it is an appropriate line for your work. Is it the type of material that you would use on your job? For example, if it is something that is for inexpensive contract use and you are only doing very exclusive offices, perhaps this catalog does not deserve to be in your library. If you intend to keep it, keep it in a section apart from your usual sources. If you are doing residential work, contract catalogs which require quantity purchases perhaps are not right for your studio.

Review each line. If it is appropriate to your work, consider some basic ground rules. Does the product meet your quality standard? Is it something that you would be pleased as a designer to recommend? I suggest that you find out a great deal about the product quality. We insist that our designers see the products, either by a personal visit to the showrooms or factories or by seeing the products within another installation. We ask our sales people to give us a list of places where we can see their products in use. We also discuss the products with other designers. signers.

Is the product manufactured within a reasonable distance from the studio or jobs? Freight and administration problems make bringing things from a long distance expensive. We, as designers, have to realize that products that are available from a similar geographic area or a close geographic area, are much easier to work with and to handle successfully on a project.

I have noticed that many interior design firms are increasingly using more neighborhood sources, especially for custom products.

Can this company handle special product work? Many production lines are not in a position to stop or change products as the designers require. If you want something special, you may be forced to go to a smaller, more flexible company. Check this before considering changing any product or doing any special design work with an existing product. These variations can not only be expensive, but

180

they can also be disastrous if using companies that are not set up to do special design work.

Once we have decided that this product is suitable, we find out who at the factory we can talk to about it. We want to know a person whom we can contact at any time during working hours who can answer any of the questions that we have pertaining to the new product. Very often, salesmen are not available except in the evenings or on Saturdays, and they are hard to reach.

The more familiar with factories and general production problems you are, the easier it is to talk to factory people. I was raised in my father's furniture factory and helped him run it for a long time. What I learned makes it easy for me to go into other factories and discuss changes and alterations. Establish a personal contact at the factory, someone you can talk to about any problem that comes along.

Most us prefer to deal on a basis of an open account. If you have acquired a good credit standing for your company, an open account should be available. It is important to establish your credit at the beginning of a relationship. If you wait until you place an order it could delay delivery.

Review your sources at least once a year. Five or ten years ago the manufacturers with showrooms in the D&D Building in New York, L.A.'s Pacific Design Center, Chicago's American Mart, and Philadelphia's Marketplace were completely different. Some of the buildings are now converted to other uses; others were only plans and blue prints. The market has changed, the sources moved or went out of business because it became uneconomical to produce certain types of products.

Make each firm you deal with your ally, not just on exceptionally large projects, but on every project. Some firms have laboratories and testing equipment which can help you analyze functional problems or can do a chemical analysis for you.

When I have a project with specific needs, I enlist my resource firm. I define the problem, the type of client, the probably maintenance as well as the budget and design requirements. With this rundown, the company and I come up with a product recommendation to work in that situation. Their knowledge is an asset, something I could not supply within my own studio, and something that helps make a professional presentation and a long lasting design.

It is our company's policy to provide a maintenance program with every job we install. We get the information from the companies we work with, for every product we purchase. Since factory guarantees are based on a maintenance procedure, review them with the company. Then make up a recommended maintenance schedule for your client: this is how to clean the lampshade, the draperies, the furniture in these situations; that is what to do in case of certain accidents; should anything else happen, call our studio. For these last problems, we find out how the manufacturer wants it handled and then make a recommendation to our client.

There are many ways of learning which manufacturers want the interior design business. I suggest you become active in your local ASID chapter's Industry Foundation programs. These let you meet companies which are interested in our special type of work. They are willing to adapt and adjust the product for us. Some firms are too large to be willing to do a special project: they want simply furniture store business.

The government has put a lot of new regulations on the products we handle. Your best sources of regulation information are the companies you purchase from. They are required to supply you with flameproofing certificates and other information needed to meet state requirements. You, as designer, are responsible for every product you specify, so be sure to keep abreast of state regulations.

Quality is a commodity. A lot of excellent designs are still made by high quality sources, but some are costly. At times, budget compels us to go to a mass market product.

Even so, discriminating clients will sometimes refuse to accept products from the mass market. So I make a point of having someone from my firm work over these pieces, checking the finish, the upholstery details, and the overall quality.

On occasion, we have been stuck with expensive repair bills for mass produced furniture. Now I try to build in a safety cushion in each project where we use mass market products. In a project where I needed 12 reproduction chairs, one source offered the chair at $1,100 each and a source from the mass market had it in the $300-$400 range. I added about 20% to the price I quoted for the mass market chair to cover any adjustments or refinements that needed to be done when the chair reached my studio. Quoting clients a variable price—the chair will be $380 to $450—gives me leeway within the budget to make up any shortcoming. I am pleased because the client has an excellent quality product and my client is pleased because he was never aware of the shortcoming.

Clients have no idea what happens behind the scenes, and if a job is run smoothly, they shouldn't have any idea. They are hiring us for a professional job. Coordinating the project is the key to professionalism.

Are your purchase orders easy to understand? Review purchase order procedures, either with another design firm or with some of your sources. You are not dealing with another designer, but with a contractor or manufacturer who may not be familiar with your vocabulary. It is easy to say that a firm that wants your business should learn your language, but we must also recognize that the talents that go into production scheduling and manufacturing are not the same talents interior designers must have. Try to find out what they need to know from you in order to give you what you want.

I have learned to be very careful, to recheck to see that everything is properly sidemarked and identified. We have purchase order numbers which relate to our individual order numbers, and our in-house communication is as simple as we can possibly make it. We also have a required follow-up procedure. If we have not heard from a company within 10 days with an acknowledgement or some comment, we either call or write again. No purchase order simply lies in the files waiting for something to happen. We have a set day each week to review purchase orders, but every problem regarding those orders is handled on the day it is received. You may be tempted to lay things aside in hopes they will take care of themselves. Don't. It doesn't happen. The longer a problem goes untended, the greater the difficulties become.

Use the telephone whenever possible when placing orders, but always follow a call with a formal purchase order in writing. We are a verbal people, but when it comes to the mathematical measurements required in the design field, we need to see it in writing.

In the past several years, I have been doing many workshops pertaining to communication between sources and designers. In preparation for one of these workshops, I asked Mr. A. W. Pease, Jr., Vice President of Payne & Company, to give me some of his comments as to ways that we might improve communication between designers and sources. The following is the outline that he gave me. I

184

think that many of these are very applicable to our situation, and I think it helps to review them. You will understand more how the sources feel about designer communication. This type of list could be worked out with each and every kind of material we order, whether it be furniture or other products, but you will see the general information structure that he has established here.

1. Do not duplicate orders by placing them twice. For example, by telephone and mail. If you do telephone an order and follow it up with a written order, be sure that the written order is clearly marked "confirming previously telephoned order." Many sources handle hundreds of orders per day for a similar number of customers and cannot be responsible for identifying identical orders coming to them via two methods of communication. Likewise, if an order is mailed and you later decide to telephone, make it clear to your sources that the same order you are telephoning is coming by mail so the source can watch for it and avoid duplication.

2. When ordering, specify by the complete identification or specification. Omissions or brevity may lead to misunderstanding, or leave the supplier in doubt.

3. When inquiring about an order already placed, always mention what the order called for (rather than just giving an order number). It helps expedite in the event the original order was never received by the supplier.

4. In times of ascending prices, it is well to add from 5% to 10% to your selling price as a protection against a possible unknown cost increase. Most suppliers—if their products are selling and their inventory turning—do in these times have to ship on a basis of price prevailing at time of shipment. If a substantial quantity is involved it is important to get a firm quotation from the source.

5. When requesting a cutting of present stock, advise

the yardage that will be needed. Without knowing what your requirement may be, the source cannot promise that the same stock will be available when a definite order is received. However, most sources will reserve specific yardage for a reasonable length of time if they know what your requirement will be.

6. When attempting to match fabric to paint, or vice versa, always obtain the fabric before painting. A small cutting from present stock can be deceiving. In a larger piece the intensity of color may make an entirely different appearance. Therefore, the safe practice is to actually have the fabric yardage needed and work from that in arriving at the paint color.

7. When ordering fabrics for draperies, indicate the size and number of cut lengths needed. For many logical reasons, suppliers cannot always ship a specific requirement in one length—and, unfortunately, not always completely free of defects. However, if the source has the detail of the requirement it is possible to expedite shipment.

8. When necessary to match a fabric, submit a cutting to match to. Even though you may be ordering small yardage to supplement a recent shipment (to complete a job) the supplier may not be able to furnish the requirement from the same piece or dye lot of the first shipment. A few suppliers, usually those with short lines, may keep a cutting to show what was shipped in the first instance, but most firms do not keep such records.

9. When using a reversible fabric for COM orders, carefully instruct the manufacturer or fabricator which side to use as the "face side." It is commonly assumed that the "face side" is that side which is rolled or folded to the inside. That is not always true! Be sure your fabricator knows what you are considering the "face side."

186

10. Check cuttings submitted with invoices. When a supplier drop ships to a destination other than your own, most firms attach a cutting to the invoice that goes to you to show what has been shipped. You have a responsibility to check that cutting for accuracy. Do it promptly before any fabrication can be started.

11. Identify COM goods sent to a processor. Write your processor telling him what to expect, from whom it is coming, what processing is to be done and to whom it should be shipped when completed. You would be surprised how many times COM goods are sent in here (usually for quilting, flameproofing or fabrication in our workroom) and the fabric sits here for days and days because no one bothered to tell us what is to be done with it. Then suddenly someone frantically wants it finished even before we start.

12. When a certificate of flameproofing is required for fabric to be flameproofed, request the certificate at the time the fabric order is placed. The detail is carried out much more smoothly than when the certificate is requested weeks or months later—and is, in fact, sometimes difficult to get.

13. When requesting memo samples, give as much information as possible. It helps the person selecting the samples to give you the most satisfactory response. A broad description—and knowing the ultimate end use—helps towards making the most intelligent and pleasing selection.

14. When remitting, list the invoices being paid. Some suppliers furnish duplicate invoices, one copy to be returned with your remittance. It helps to identify—to maintain a mutual understanding of an account.

15. Make returns promptly. If there is cause for merchandise to be returned, advise your supplier promptly

and make the return promptly. It will avoid irritation, possible confusion and perhaps further inconvenience to you. Always advise the supplier why the return.

16. Keep the lines of communication open with the supplier's credit department. If you are unable to pay within terms—notify. Don't neglect. In spite of having a reputation of having ice water in their veins, credit managers are generally very reasonable people anxious to help you in every reasonable way they can. Keeping them informed of your situation and intentions is the best way to gain their greatest cooperation.

BOOK LIST

A Guide to Business Principles and Practices for Interior Designers, Harry Seigel, CPA, Whitney, 1968, N.Y.

This Business of Interior Design, Harry Seigel, CPA, Whitney, 1976, N.Y.

The Blue Book of Broadminded Business Behavior, Auren Uris, Thomas Y. Crowell, 1977, N.Y.

Management—A Systems & Contingency Analysis of Management Functions, Harold Kovitz, Ayril O'Donnel, McGraw-Hill, N.Y., 1976.

Legal Guide for the Visual Artist, Tad Crawford, Hawthorne Books, N.Y., 1977.

Legal Forms for the Designer, Lee Epstein, N & E Hellman, N.Y., 1977.

Huddling—The Informal Way to Management Success, V. Dallas Merrell, AMACOM, N.Y., 1979.

Reality in Advertising, Rosser Reeves, Alfred A. Knopf, N.Y., 1976.

Dictionary of Business & Finance, Donald T. Clark & Bert A. Gottfried, Thomas Y. Crowell, N.Y., 1967.

Essentials of Managerial Finance, J. Fred Weston, Eugene F. Brigham, The Dryden Press, Hinsdale, Ill., 1978.

Management, Tasks, Responsibilities, Practices, Peter F. Drucher, Harper & Row, Publishers, N.Y., 1974.

People & Performance: The Best of Peter Drucher on Management, Peter F. Drucher, Harper's College Press, N.Y., 1977.

Legal Handbook for Small Business, Marc. J. Lane, AMACOM, N.Y., 1977.

How to Advertise, Kenneth Roman and Jane Maas, St. Martins Press, N.Y., 1976.

Work in America, The Decade Ahead, Clark Kerr, Jerome M. Rosow, Van Nostrand, Reinhold, N.Y., 1979.

Accounting Handbook for Non-Accountants, Clarence B. Nickerson, Cahners, Boston, Mass., 1975.

How to Market Professional Design Services, Gerre L. Jones, McGraw-Hill, 1973.

This Business of Art, Diane Cochrane, Watson-Guptill, N.Y., 1978.

Your Career in Business, Walter Hoving, Tiffany & Co., N.Y., 1977.

The Art of Design Management, Thomas F. Schutte, Tiffany & Co., N.Y., 1975.

Creative Communication for a Successful Design Practice, Stephen A. Klement, AIA, Whitney, 1977.

Current Techniques in Architectural Practice, Class-Koehler, McGraw-Hill, 1976.

190

About the author . . .

Mary Knackstedt, a professional designer and widely known lecturer based in Harrisburg and New York City, has been concentrating on the planning of interiors for profitable business management since 1958. Her problem-solving techniques for an impressive list of credits in business, institutional and residential areas became the dynamic subjects for lectures and seminars organized for prestige industry groups and schools including ASID, AIA, NHFL, Young Presidents Organization, Drexel University (Philadelphia), New School for Social Research (New York). The subjects subsequently provided the core of her best selling motivational Cassette Tape Program.

President of the Pennsylvania East Chapter ASID and a member of its National Committee of Professional Practices, Mary Knackstedt is a key lecturer at its regional and national conferences as well as business columnist and contributing editor for The Designer Magazine. Since 1970 she has also been a management consultant turning new or faltering companies into profitable ventures through systematic construction techniques.

Her formal design education began at Pratt and continued through many specialized courses of study in business as well as design. After apprenticing under several interior designers, she opened her own firm, Mary K. Interiors Inc., and has since been providing full interior design services for an impressive list of national corporations, professional, and private clients.